One-on-one Meetings are Underrated;

Group Meetings Waste Time

One-on-one Meetings are Underrated;

Group Meetings Waste Time

By Lawrence Krubner

Contents

Example 1

What does my mom get for dinner? (Software is making hospitals worse.)

This is a book about work, but I'd like to start with a funny, personal story that I think communicates something about how to handle software bug reports.

My mom, who is 93 years old, was at Mount Sinai hospital for a week, with an infected foot. She got lots of antibiotics and I'm pleased to say she recovered quickly. I went over on a Monday, and was told they were going to send her home the next day.

Boredom is the only universal condition at a hospital (sometimes mixed with terror). My mom was in a room with 2 other patients and she didn't have anywhere to go, and nothing to see, nor did the nurses allow her out into the hallway, except when I was with her, so I went there each day and we'd go for a long walk down the hallways.

These days hospitals are more and more dependent on software, yet the bureaucratic confusion never seems to end. I actually think software makes things worse, in that the rigidity of software accentuates the rough edges of bureaucracy, as opposed to the old days, when bureaucracies were overseen by an army of secretaries, who could informally adjust a given process when that process was in danger of producing an obviously stupid result.

I wish hospitals were the kind of market where innovative software startups could bring cool new ideas to improve processes overall, but sadly the opposite is true. Over the last 10 years, more and more every year, Epic Software has become a monopoly that has taken over the internal workings of every hospital. And, like with any monopoly, they've become less and less innovative, because they no longer need to compete. They charge tens of millions of dollars, yet they leave hospitals with an inflexible system that's much worse than what the hospital had before.

I ran into this on that Monday night at Mount Sinai, my mom's final night at the hospital. I was worried about my mom getting dinner. Every previous night she had been skipped over — I couldn't figure out why. Since I was there, I felt I could fix the situation.

In the hallway I saw the food delivery woman, who was probably about 60 years old. She was pushing her giant metal cart with about 40 meals, for all the people in that section. I went over to her and asked for food for my mom.

"Who's your mom?" she asked.

"Blanche Krubner."

A thick stack of papers, stapled together, sat atop the cart, with information on each patient. She flipped through this till she found my mom.

"Oh, okay," she said. "Mrs Krubner, right? Okay, she is listed as 'Restricted Carbohydrates.' Alright, alright, alright. I can give you this."

She gave me a plate with fried chicken, some mashed potatoes, and some stewed carrots. I took this to my mom, who sat down and ate it. For hospital food, she said, it was not bad.

When my mom was done eating I took her plate and tray and walked out into the hallway. I found a dolly where the trays seemed to collect, so I set mom's tray there and went back to her room.

A long while passed, almost an hour, and then the food lady came into the room, bringing food to the two other patients who were sharing the room with my mom. I didn't realize it at first, but the food lady seemed to be puzzled about my mom's food situation.

My mom was sitting in her chair reading a murder mystery. The food lady had an iPad with her with some information about each patient, and after a few moments, she seemed to make a big discovery.

"Oh, okay, I see," said the food lady. "Your mom is NPO. That's why I cannot give her any food."

"What?" I asked, confused.

"She is not allowed any food." The food lady held up the iPad so I could see the screen, which also showed the Epic logo, so I knew which software company had created the system that the hospital used. "She's NPO, that means the doctors don't want her to eat."

"Why?" I asked.

"Maybe she is going for surgery in the morning?" suggested the food lady.

"I'm fairly sure I would know if my mom was going for surgery in the morning," I said.

"Who knows why?" The food lady shrugged. "But she must go 24 hours without food, before it happens."

"But she had breakfast," I said. "And they fed her lunch."

"Oh, that's bad," said the food lady. "They shouldn't have done that. Someone's going to get in trouble."

"But she just ate dinner," I said.

"What?" The food lady was shocked. "Where did she get dinner?"

"You gave it to me," I said.

"When?" she asked.

"About an hour ago," I said. "I walked up to you and asked for food for my mom and you gave me a meal."

"I did that?" She seemed nervous. "Why would I do that? This lady is NPO! She cannot have any food before her surgery!"

"She isn't going for surgery!" I insisted. "She is being discharged in the morning. And then we are going to her favorite restaurant and she is going to order the salmon, which is her favorite meal."

"Wait, wait, wait," the food lady was on the edge of panic. "Something is wrong. She is NPO. She should not eat! Why didn't you tell me she was NPO?"

"I have no idea what that means," I said. "And also, I didn't know she was NPO. I thought she was 'Restricted Carbohydrates'."

"What are you talking about?" asked the food lady.

"On that paper print out that you showed me earlier," I explained. "It said my mom was 'Restricted Carbohydrates.'"

"No, that's impossible," she said, "They always say the same thing. They have to."

We went out to the food cart and she got the thick stack of papers. We looked at them together, and sure enough, the paper stack said that my mom was 'Restricted Carbohydrates.'"

"Wait, now, wait, I mean, wait, I mean, what is this?" she asked. And she checked the iPad again, where it said my mom was NPO. "Well, why does it say she's NPO here, if it says she's 'Restricted Carbohydrates' over here?"

"Um?" I was baffled. "I have no idea? I don't know anything about your hospital? I don't know anything about the paper printout, or the software? I don't know what NPO means and I don't even really know what 'Restricted Carbohydrate' means? But also, Epic is a money grubbing monopoly that sucks $100 million out of any hospital chain in exchange for bad software that has many problems?"

"You say what now?" she asked, looking at me funny, or rather, looking at me as if I was kind of funny, but not in a good way.

"I don't know the answer to your question," I said simply.

"It's supposed to say the same thing!" she said angrily. "If

Epic says she's NPO, then the paper should say she's NPO!"

"Software sucks?" I offered, which is the shortest way I can summarize my 22 year career in software.

"Well," she shrugged. "Now I ain't got any idea what she should eat!"

"It's okay," I said. "She leaves tomorrow."

"Good!" she shouted, but not in the happy 'I hope you feel better' kind of way that most of the nurses often say. More like, "Good riddance, you fake NPO woman!"

The food lady left. My mom missed all the drama and was still sitting in the chair reading her murder mystery. I sat down next to her and she looked up at me.

"Did you get enough to eat?" I asked.

"Yes, thank you," she said. "For hospital food, the dinner was fairly good."

"I'm glad you liked it," I said. "And I'm really glad you won't be here tomorrow."

"Oh, me too honey!" she said. "I'll be so pleased to get out of here!"

"Yes, especially since this hospital will never give you any food again."

"What?" she asked.

"I mean, I'll be so happy to take you to your favorite restaurant!" I said.

"Me too!" she said.

Of course, the next day we ran into the same slow bureaucracy that seems to haunt every hospital. I was told the doctor would check her in the morning and I should arrive by 10 AM and take her home, so I got there at 10 AM. They then told me the doctor was running late and would arrive at 1:30 PM. But the doctor didn't arrive until 3:30 PM. They only needed a few minutes to look at mom and approve her release. We finally got out of there a bit after 4 PM.

Thankfully, we did get out of there, and we did go to mom's favorite restaurant, where there was no confusion about whether my mom was NPO or Restricted Carbohydrates or whether she was going for surgery. My mom ordered the salmon and she was very happy.

Now, this story is funny, in its way, but I also think its an excellent example of the correct way to handle a bug report if you are a manager: as much as possible, go with the person who makes the complaint, look at what they see on screen, and try to fully understand why they think there is a problem. Talk with them one-on-one. I went with the food cart lady to her cart, we compared what she saw on her iPad with what was on the paper printout. I hope there is someone on the tech team at Mount Sinai who can do exactly what I did, see the problem, and then get to the root of it.

One-on-one conversations are magical. They are often the best way to discover the truth of a complicated situation.

Having said that, let's look at another bug report, one made worse by the laziness or dishonesty of someone on the tech team. This next story is far more serious.

Example 2

Bug reports, dishonesty, and direct feedback

In 2011 I was working at a travel site that gathered up travel deals from the major air, cruise and hotel companies and then promoted them on the site. The whole tech team was just six engineers, and Sonia was our project manager and also our entire QA team.

One week, after we pushed out some new code, Sonia tested the web site – informally clicking around, looking for any mistakes.

Sonia: I don't think I'm seeing all of the travel deals that I should be seeing.

Me: What is missing?

Sonia: I need to research this.

Everything looked okay to me, but I didn't know all of the conditions that might impinge on our broadcast of travel deals. Sometimes we'd get new deals from Delta Airlines or Viking

Cruise Ships, but sometimes we were supposed to hold those deals, and only unleash them on a particular date. Should they be visible on the dates in the future that Sonia was testing in the search tool? She wasn't sure so she went over to the Travel Deals Team and consulted with them.

A while later she came back over to where the tech team sat, and now she was convinced there was a problem with our search engine.

Sonia: See, if I search for Bermuda I see certain deals, and if I search for Saint Vincent I see certain deals, and if I add in a specific date range I can still see all of those deals, but if I instead search for "Caribbean" then three deals disappear.

Me: We include Bermuda in the category of Caribbean?

Sonia: Yes, we do.

Me: Okay, well, we should create a ticket and someone should figure out what's wrong.

Sonia: I'll create the ticket. How many hours do you estimate this will take?

Me: This has to be an exploration ticket, because the problem could be in many different areas of the code. It could be a problem in the database, or in our search tool Solr, or it could be in the actual frontend website code. I mean, who knows? Someone needs to explore.

Sonia: Okay, how much time will this exploration take?

Me: Let's say four hours.

For a problem like this, where the bug could be almost anywhere in our system, we would create exploration tickets, where the goal was simply to do research and discover what the real problem was. Then, once we knew what the problem was, we could create another ticket, to cover the work needed to fix the real problem.

Sonia created the ticket, put down an estimate of four hours, and then the following week, when the next work-sprint started (our work was organized into two week sprints), the ticket was picked up by my co-worker Jerry. About 90% of all the search code had been written by Jerry, so if anyone was going to find out the cause of the problem, it would probably be him. Certainly, he knew the search code better than anyone else.

The next day came and I knew this ticket would be Jerry's first priority and very quickly I saw that he'd marked the ticket as "done" with a note that said "There was no actual bug." Jerry lived in another city, and was working from home, so I reached out to him and we set up a video conversation.

Me: So, you had a chance to look at the problem that Sonia found? The travel deals that aren't being listed when people do certain searches?

Jerry: Yeah, no problem, she was just searching for the wrong things.

Me: What does that mean?

Jerry: She was combining too many search terms. She confused herself.

Me: Well, is our search engine supposed to support all of the search terms that she was using?

Jerry: Sure, but if you combine all of it, then certain deals won't show up.

Me: Are you sure? Sonia is very careful. She doesn't usually say some software quirk is a bug unless it really is a bug.

Jerry: The code is very complex and has to take into account dozens of special circumstances. Sonia just didn't get it. The deals that didn't show up were not supposed to show up.

Me: Sonia herself has, over the years, defined most of the special circumstances that you reference. She defined them and then you turned them into code. It doesn't seem likely that she would not be aware of the special circumstances.

Jerry: Sure, but no one can keep track of all the different ways those special circumstances can combine. Fifty special circumstances can have tens of thousands of combinations. In this case the combinations were just too complicated for her. I checked the Solr configuration and everything is correct.

Me: Okay, thanks for doing that. I appreciate it.

I told Sonia the good news, that there was no actual bug, but she was suspicious of that answer. She spent the next hour running various searches, and taking copious notes, and then consulting with the Travel Deals Team to be sure some searches were not showing up. Then she asked me to review what she'd found, which I did, and I acknowledged there did seem to be a real problem.

After all that, she was ready to phrase things in a new way, which might overcome Jerry's objections: even if this problem wasn't exactly a software bug, strictly defined, there were deals that the Travel Deals Team wanted to have appear on our website, in conjunction with certain search terms, and yet these deals were not appearing. If this was because of an unusual combination of special circumstances, then some of those special circumstances were in need of modification.

At this point three things happened:

1. Sonia created a new ticket.

2. Jerry almost instantly marked it as "done," again with the comment that there was no actual problem.

3. I got angry.

The situation had morphed from a technical problem to an attitude problem. I didn't like Jerry's tone, so I asked for another one-on-one chat with him over video.

Me: Sonia has devoted considerable time to documenting a problem with the travel search.

Jerry: Again, I've explained this to you, there is no actual problem. It's the way she's combining special circumstances, in ways that limit which deals can appear on the site.

Me: That doesn't matter. There are deals that the Travel Deals Team wants to have on the site, and those deals are not appearing. So whatever code you wrote to handle whatever previous special circumstances might have been important in the past, that code is now going to change.

Jerry: But I already told you...

Me: Doesn't matter! We are trying to sell some deals! The Travel Deals Team wants these deals to appear on the site! We are going to change the code to be sure these deals show up!

Jerry (with a heavy sigh): Okay, okay, okay, whatever, okay? Whatever. This is stupid, but I'll look into it.

Me: No, don't bother. I'm going to handle this ticket myself.

By this point I'd lost faith in Jerry. I wasn't sure he was working in good faith, and worse, I couldn't trust what he was saying to me. Maybe he was feeling lazy or maybe he was trying to defend the code he'd written in the past. Either way, something kept him from fixing this problem the first time he looked at it, and now I wanted a better understanding of what was going wrong.

As it turned out, the problem was subtle and very deep. The next day, I spent several hours tracking it down. In the end, the problem was in our configuration for Solr, our search tool. The configuration was wrong. Working closely with Sonia, I fixed the problem, and then we ran some tests in a test sandbox environment, to convince ourselves that my update to the code would really fix the problem. The next day we pushed out the new code and thankfully the problem was fixed.

That ended the software problem, but it didn't end the attitude issue. To have healthy team dynamics we had to be able to trust each other, and I wanted to make that clear to Jerry. We had another one-on-one video chat (I would have preferred to have this meeting in-person, but Jerry lived in another city).

Me: I fixed this issue with the search tool and those travel deals that were not appearing on the site.

Jerry: What was the issue?

Me: There was a mistake in the Solr configuration that affected how data was copied over from our main database.

Jerry: Well, okay, good job. I'm glad you figured that out.

Me: I want to ask you something. When you originally took the ticket, I noticed that you were fairly quick to mark it "done." Do you remember how long you spent on it?

Jerry: I looked at the Solr configuration, but everything

looked correct to me.

Me: Right, sure, but how much time did that take you?

Jerry: About 15 minutes.

Me: The ticket was estimated to take four hours.

Jerry: Why would I waste four hours on a ticket if I could do it in 15 minutes?

Me: But you didn't really do it, did you?

Jerry: I mean, come on, I did what I could to see if there was a problem.

Me: Did you read any of Sonia's documentation? In 15 minutes?

Jerry: Maybe?

Me: Here is the thing. Sonia is the best project manager that I've ever worked with. She is very careful. She documents everything. If she says there is a problem, then there is almost certainly a problem.

Jerry: Yeah, yeah, yeah, I see where you are going with this, but no one is perfect. I'm sure she makes mistakes sometimes.

Me: She didn't make a mistake this time.

Jerry: Okay, this time I made a mistake, what do you want?

Me: I want you to take bug reports seriously, when they come from a trusted source.

Jerry: Okay, whatever, from now on I'll take all of Sonia's bug reports seriously.

Me: That means reading all of her documentation.

Jerry: Right, right, sure.

Me: I feel like you're not really listening to me.

Jerry: I am listening to you! For god's sake, what do you want? I'm not doing anything else right now. I'm sitting here listening to you.

Me: I need you to understand this. You will not ever do anything like this again.

Jerry: Yeah, yeah, I already said that, I'll check out Sonia's bug reports, yeah.

Me: I mean about me. Don't do it again.

Jerry: Do what? What are you talking about?

Me: Don't give me your assurance that you've examined a piece of code and you are certain there is no bug, when in fact you did not examine the code, you did not examine the bug report, you didn't even understand what the bug report actually said. Don't mark a ticket as "done" when you haven't even started on it.

Jerry: I didn't want to waste time on a non-issue.

Me: You ended up wasting Sonia's time and also my time. And you kept travel deals off the site for several days when we could have been making money off them.

Jerry (heavy sigh): Yes, okay, that was bad on my part. I get that. I apologize. Okay? I apologize.

Me: I appreciate that, but the most important thing is that, in the future, I can trust you when you say "There is no bug."

Jerry: Yes, okay, I get that. I need to be more careful.

Me: If you pull a ticket that authorizes you to do four hours of exploration, then use some of that time and do an honest exploration.

Jerry: Yes, okay, I promise. I made a mistake, I will handle it better next time.

Me: Okay, great. Thank you for talking to me about this.

And thankfully, he really did get it, and we never needed to have a conversation like that again.

It is possible to talk to people directly, honestly, firmly, and respectfully, to communicate how you expect them to work with you. Please note what I didn't do: I didn't use swear words, or raise my voice, nor did I say anything personal about their character or work ethic, other than how it applied in this specific case. You might think I've cleaned up this dialogue for the book, but no. I do not ever use curse words in a business context, and I recommend this, since any use of curse words carries the risk that people will feel you are being disrespectful.

Some managers are afraid of this kind of direct, honest conversation. They fall back to a style of communication that is much more passive aggressive. I've seen cases where, after an incident like this, the manager will send an email to the whole team, and without any reference to the original incident that is motivating the email, they will write "If you get a bug report, please investigate it thoroughly." Most of the time, such communication is a mistake. Every worker is different, and they will make different kinds of mistakes, and your feedback to them needs to be specific to them. Maybe you have one worker who dismisses bug reports, and another worker who comes in late to work, and another worker who leaves food on their desk overnight, and another worker who never tests their own code. Does that mean you should send four different emails, advising the whole team to take bug reports seriously, come in on time, don't leave food out overnight, and test your own work? No, the number of possible mistakes is infinite, so you'd have to send an infinite amount of email. Worse, people tend to ignore such emails – if the workers know that you're afraid to confront them, then they know they can continue in their bad habits with few consequences. Instead, you need to have one-on-one conversations with each worker, and you need to give them feedback that is specific to them.

Some managers feel that direct, honest communication can sometimes feel a bit aggressive, but that shouldn't matter. As a manager you have an obligation to protect the team, and that means you need to get each person on the team to do their work and to report on that work honestly. You can engage in direct, honest communication while also being respectful. You don't need to swear. You don't need to raise your voice. You might be angry but you don't need to express that. Keep the focus on what matters: the long-term health of the team depends on everyone doing their job, and being honest about what they've done.

Context matters. My conversation with Jerry was respectful because it was a private, one-on-one conversation. If I had addressed him like that in a group setting, then he'd have more reason to feel attacked, and therefore he'd have more reason to get defensive. In that case there would be less chance of him actually listening to me. All such feedback should be given privately, in one-on-one conversations. If you want someone to change their behavior, this is always the best form of conversation.

Example 3

Your client says they want one thing, but they really want something else

In the year 2000 I was just starting my career, by creating small websites for small businesses. This was long before the era of automated site-builders like WordPress or Wix or Squarespace, so the only way for a small business to get a website was to hire someone like me, to build the site by hand.

One of my early clients was a woman named Tonia, who sold vitamins. A friend had put me in touch, I met with her once, and now I was meeting with her a second time to show her some designs that I thought would work for her e-commerce site. I had come up with several designs, including a one-column, two-column, three-column, and four-column design. I'd randomly, and without much thought, grabbed some photos off the Web, and used them as placeholders to show where images could go in the design.

Me: So, as you can see, I've got these different designs, and I think each could work for you. The one-column design puts the emphasis on the image. The three and four column designs allow us to put more scientific data up front.

Tonia (pointing to the image of a tropical island, the main image of the one-column design): I really like this one.

Me (a little surprised): Oh? Okay, so you'd like to put the emphasis on the image?

Tonia: Yes.

Me: Okay, I can work with that. So we need to find a really great image that can fit in this space. It's the dominant image on the page, and it is the first thing that your customers will see, so whatever you choose, it has to make an impression.

Tonia (a little upset): Wait, we can't use this image?

Me (confused): What image? The image of the tropical island?

Tonia: Yes, like I said, I really love the image.

Me: Um, sure. I could track down the rights for commercial use. Interesting idea.

Tonia: It's such a beautiful tropical island.

Me: Yes, it is a beautiful scene.

Tonia (laughing): I really wish I was there right now!

Me: Yes, I know what you mean!

Tonia: Okay, so we will go with that.

Me: Sure, I'll get the rights and we can add your text underneath it.

Tonia: No, no, no, let's add the text next to it.

Me: What?

Tonia: The thing about these vitamins is that they are processed with the best manufacturing process available with today's technology. That really is true, that's not just marketing, but it is a fact that we need to market.

Me: But if we put text next to the image, that would introduce another column.

Tonia: Great.

Me (very confused): Uhhhhhhhhhh.... Okay. So you don't want a one-column design?

Tonia: I want to put a lot of text next to the image. The scientific facts. Part of my goal with this business is to educate people about health and vitamins. I want to emphasize the facts. This is important to the business, and it's also important to me on a personal level.

Me (still confused): A lot of facts? Up front? So.... Uh.... If we went with this four-column design, we could put a lot of facts up front.

Tonia: Great, that's what I want.

Me: So you like the four-column design?

Tonia: Yes, very much. I love it.

Me: With this photo of the tropical island?

Tonia: Yes, like I said, I love it.

Back then, there was an enormous amount that I did not know, especially about handling clients. Tonia lacked the graphic design skills to analyze what she needed and figure out what kind of design would suit her needs, so when I talked to her about columns I was, in a sense, speaking a foreign language. But she fell in love with the photo that I used in the one-column design. After some conversation, I eventually figured out what she really wanted, which was the four-column design that allowed her to put a large number of facts up front where the customer could see them. The image of the tropical island was shrunk down, and occupied only one of the columns.

Sometimes clients, customers, users, and co-workers are unable to tell you what they want. Or rather, they know what they want, but they don't know how those desires might translate into your professional language. It's up to you to figure out the translation. Helpful in that regard, a long one-on-one conversation can allow you to test assumptions, perhaps confront them with the outcomes of some of the things they seem to say: "If we do this, then we end up with this. Are you sure this is what you really want?" And then it's either yes or no.

By no means am I minimizing the difficulties of User Experience research. Sometimes you need to study the behavior of millions of users, and in those cases you'll have to use other techniques, since you can't have an individual conversation with millions of people. But even when dealing with millions of users, you might decide to do an ethnographic study of a small sample of them, at which point you are back to doing a long, one-on-one conversation.

Great project managers understand this. Terrible project managers will expect the other teams in a company to figure out what they need, make a request, and then define "success" as giving that other team what they requested, rather than what they wanted. Great project managers know a process of translation is often needed between the different teams in an organization, as each team speaks a different professional language.

I have seen companies destroyed when crucial relationships, which needed to be close, were instead relegated to the legalities of written contracts. Don't let this happen to your company. One-on-one conversations are an amazingly flexible tool that proves useful again and again, in a great diversity of situations. If you are a leader and you run into a problem, one question you should always ask yourself is "Can this problem be solved if I have a one-on-one conversation with someone?" This is true both within the team and with external third parties or clients.

Introduction

Since 1999 I've been the technical co-founder or team lead at three startups, I've been a consultant to perhaps thirty entrepreneurs, and I've spoken to more than a hundred. In the areas of finance, hiring, and styles of leadership, I've seen what works well versus what leads to failure. In this short book, I will cover some pragmatic issues:

- How to hire
- How to project manage
- How to organize meetings, and with whom

The focus, obviously, is on communication, for better and for worse.

Many of the books aimed at entrepreneurs are overly optimistic and full of simplistic advice. By contrast, this book aims for realism, acknowledging that building a company is difficult and stressful work. I include both stories of success and stories of failure so as to make clear that both are possible. Moreover, we need to acknowledge that when things go badly the defeat is often self-imposed and easy to avoid. Sometimes entrepreneurs ask me, "What if Google decides to compete with us? They will crush us!" And yet I've never seen this fear come true. Rather, self-sabotage is considerably more common. If you can avoid irrational, self-destructive behavior, then you're already doing better than most entrepreneurs.

This book is aimed at entrepreneurs and managers of small- to medium-sized firms — in particular, those with less than 500 employees. If you are in the rare situation of overseeing explosive, order-of-magnitude growth every year, then I recommend a book by Reid Hoffman called *Blitzscaling*. By contrast, this book is for the more common case of a firm enjoying normal growth, or perhaps trying to bounce back after an unfortunate event.

When it comes to leadership and management advice, the law of diminishing returns sets in fast. There are some basic ideas that are useful to know, but take all such advice lightly and adapt it to your own use. Some other business books try to offer detailed programs and step-by-step practices that they insist you must implement exactly, but I've found that past a certain point the burden of such practices costs more than any benefits that you might derive from them. This book will demand less requirements on your time.

Chapter 1

A simple message: smaller meetings are more productive than larger meetings

Back in the 1980s, when he was President of Intel, Andy Grove wrote a book called *High Output Management*, and he went into some detail about the importance of one-on-ones, which for him were a regular practice during which his reports could come in and talk about any subject. This gave rise to a new management fad, and some companies now mandate that every manager must have "one–on–ones" with their workers. When you force a manager to do this, some of them bring a bad attitude into their meetings and things generally don't go well.

Some people love Grove's book whereas others feel he took simple concepts and made them sound overly complicated. I'm in the latter group. That's especially true when it comes to one-on-one meetings. I don't think it is wise to build a cult around this, or any, management practice. For my part, I think there are a handful of good ideas that tend to make management better, but these ideas should be practiced as simply as possible.

Therefore, I'm not advocating for mandatory or even regular one-on-ones. What I am advocating is that you, personally, should consider the benefits of very small meetings, containing just one or two people, besides yourself. That is, you should consider how much this benefits you and your team. When you keep meetings as small as possible, you are allowing as many people as possible to continue to do their work, without being disturbed, because they are not in the meeting. When you need specific information, just invite the people who can give you that information, and when you need to give information to one person, meet with just that one person.

When I need to announce something to a large group, I can send an email to everyone, or send a message to a whole channel on Slack, or send a group text on WhatsApp — I'm lucky to have an abundance of options nowadays. I don't need to get them all together in a room. Even if I thought gathering people together was the best strategy, how would I handle the fact that on any particular day I might have key workers who are out sick, or taking care of a sick child, or working remotely? Do I send them an email? Have a one-on-one meeting with them later? If so, why not make that my primary strategy? The overall approach of "email for announcements, one-on-one meetings for serious conversations" has the advantage that, as a strategy, it scales well. It's the best strategy when you have a team of five, as well as when you have a team of 500. (Obviously you don't have one-on-one meetings with each of the 500 people, but you have one-on-one meetings with the managers who oversee the teams of those 500 people.)

Some managers respond to this by arguing, "But nobody reads email." First of all, that is a weak excuse for indulging in bad managerial practices. Second, with asynchronous communication, such as email or Slack, you can send the same message several times over several days, to reinforce the idea. Third, this is precisely why you follow up with one-on-one meetings.

Aren't one-on-one meetings just a trick to manipulate workers and lie to them?

When I have discussed this issue, both online and offline, I've learned that some workers have had bad experiences with one-on-one meetings. In particular, they feel that their manager says one thing to them, when they are alone, but then the manager tells another worker something completely different, when those two meet. So the worker ends up feeling lied to and manipulated. This seems like a good reason why one-on-ones should not be mandatory. Perhaps some managers have no affinity for them.

To state the obvious, you should try to avoid hiring managers who leave workers feeling manipulated and lied to, as that will hurt the morale of the whole organization. But if you make a mistake, and you hire someone who is manipulative and cruel, it is ludicrous to suggest that one-on-one meetings are what empower them to be manipulative and cruel. If that's their personality, then they will find ways to be manipulative and cruel even if you outlaw one-on-one meetings and instead ensure that every meeting is a large group meeting.

However, there are also times when workers feel they've been lied to when they have simply misread or misheard some communication from their manager. This is an actual communication that I recently had with a freelancer I was working with, putting together some preliminary numbers for a marketing campaign:

Me: About Task 3, can you wrap this up by Thursday or Friday?

Them: I'm busy on Thursday, but I can get to Task 3 on Friday or Saturday.

Me: Are you sure you can't get this done on Friday?

Them: I don't know. I've got some things scheduled for the afternoon on Friday. I'm not sure how long that might go into the evening. But I can get it to you by Saturday afternoon, for sure.

Me: Look, this doesn't have to be perfect. Don't go overboard. Just put in what time you can on Thursday and Friday. In this case speed is more important than quality. We need this. Whatever you can do is fine.

Around 9 PM on Friday I had not heard from them, so I wrote to them again:

Me: Hey, can you please send me whatever you've got regarding Task 3?

Them: I told you, I can get it to you by Saturday afternoon.

Me: I told you the deadline was Friday.

Them: You never said the deadline was Friday.

Me: What I said was, whatever you have by this point, Friday night, is fine. I think I said that speed is more important than quality.

Them: Yeah, but you never said that Friday was the deadline.

Me: Okay, that's fine, but please send me what you have.

They sent over what they'd done so far, and it was fine. In this case, we were both a little bit in the wrong, in that neither of us made explicit what the deadline was. I thought I'd been reasonably clear that by Friday night they should just send me whatever they had, but they felt that I'd authorized them to keep going until Saturday. It's important to be very clear about expectations, otherwise workers hear what they want to hear and then sometimes feel that you misled them.

In this case, I failed to make 100% explicit that the deadline was Friday night. If I had invested a little more time into the communication, I probably would have made clear what my expectations were.

The plain truth is more powerful than some fake theory of objectivity

As a manager, you need to constantly give feedback to everyone who reports to you. Some managers mistakenly believe that in order to sound "objective" they need to always give both positive and negative feedback. Many management books actually promote this idea, but I've seen it do a lot of harm. Keep in mind you are both civilians. You are not a military colonel giving a dressing-down to a recent West Point cadet. Many of the people you will work with over the years are simply ordinary people who want ordinary careers. If they are mostly doing a good job, it is perfectly acceptable to simply tell them that they are doing a good job. If you constantly pair every positive remark with a negative one, even when a person is doing stellar work, the only possible long-term outcome is that you will damage their morale.

Occasionally you will work with someone who is ambitious, someone who is pushing themselves to improve as fast as possible. They will be hungry for all of your feedback. With them, if you wish, you can act like a military colonel giving a dressing-down to a recent West Point cadet. But these will be people who have clearly and directly asked you to mentor them.

A final point: many companies ask peers to rate one another. This may or may not be a good idea, but assuming it happens, be discreet with the information. Some managers stupidly share the peer feedback with a given employee. Please, do not ever do this. An employee's peers might bring various biases or bigotries to work; they also sometimes have an incentive to lie. Do not ever share raw feedback from peers. Always filter it down and then say what you have determined, to the best of your ability, to be true. Discretion, especially if you are on a management career track, will always be important and valued at any company, both by your reports and those who you report to.

Group meetings waste time

You might be thinking, "What is wrong with group meetings? I love group meetings. I get to talk to everyone at once, which is much more efficient than talking to each person individually. Group meetings save me a lot of time."

If you feel that way, I should warn you, I'm about to attack your deeply held beliefs. Get ready.

I once had a client who insisted that the marketing team should meet with the tech team once a month, to collaborate on the creation of marketing copy that would be informed by those who understood the technology. This was good in theory, but having less people in the room would have been way more productive. As it was, during a typical meeting we had twelve people in the room, most of whom were bored. The conversation was almost always dominated by the three most opinionated marketing people. Imagine this going on for 20 straight minutes:

Amy: Consumers are saturated with advertisements. The only way to break through is to connect with them at an emotional level. That's why we need to consider long-form advertising. We need to tell stories that really reach them.

Henry: I couldn't disagree more! Nobody has time to read a story! If you write more than ten words then you've failed.

We need a slogan that is memorable, something we can use in every ad, something that —

Amy: No! Studies show that people don't remember facts, they remember emotions. We need to *connect* with those emotions, which is why we need to consider —

Henry: Great, so we come up with ten words that pack an emotional wallop, but we don't write a damn novel! Nobody has time to read anymore, nobody —

Amy: Well I read a novel a week, sometimes two. Some people crave stories and look for narrative structure and we should give them ads that they actually enjoy and want to share with their —

Kate: No, no, you two are both wrong! People don't want stories so much as they want authenticity. We really need to forge a connection with them that feels authentic; if we hit them with an idiotic slogan or indulge in some silly fiction, that's just going to —

Henry: If we find the right ten words, it will resonate with them as authentic. That's our job, to find the ten words that *feel* authentic! What do you think we are doing here? A quick slogan gives us quick –

Kate: Authenticity is not a pack of Ramen noodles! We can't create it in five minutes, it's something that takes time to build and —

Henry: Remember the Budweiser ad, from the mid 90s, with the bullfrogs ...??? Busch pulled off a Super Bowl commercial where the *only* word spoken the entire time was "Bud-wei-ser." The ENTIRE time! Because the frogs were reciting it! To this day, my older brothers still talk about —

Amy: Oh my god, *please* for one moment try to get your head out of the clouds and think about how people actually associate ideas and products in ways that might be outside of your narrow —

Does this conversation allow the tech team to have a better understanding of the way the marketing team thinks? Yes, maybe. And if time was infinite, this would be a fun educational exercise for the tech team. Alas, time is not infinite. Such meetings encouraged the tech team to offer their non-professional opinion on matters strictly relating to marketing. Why would the marketing team want that?

A bad manager allows these meetings to drag on. A good manager ends these meetings quickly and gets people back to their real jobs. A great manager never allows such meetings to occur in the first place.

Here is a more productive method of collaboration between teams:

1. The marketing team needs to have an internal debate, and commit to one of the strategies offered by Amy, Henry, or Kate.

2. The marketing team needs to appoint one person who can act as liaison to the tech team.

3. The tech team needs to appoint one person who can act as liaison to the marketing team.

4. In both cases, the best liaison is typically the team manager, unless the integration work is being assigned to someone specific (that is, if there is one software engineer who will be expected to integrate all of the requests from the marketing team).

5. In this way, most people on both teams can focus on their real jobs, where they have professional skills, rather than spending time educating unspecialized

amateurs on a different team, or worse, listening to their unqualified opinions.

6. The occasional effort at cross-team education can be rewarding, but it should not be a regular, recurring event.

Chapter 2

When are big meetings justified?

We've discussed the value of small meetings. When are large meetings justified? Mostly in five situations:

1. Brainstorming exercises
2. Morale-building moments, such as a company party, the announcement of a big round of investment, or going out to lunch or dinner
3. Cross-functional collaboration
4. When everyone is an extrovert who hates written text
5. The all-hands, once-a-week, at startups with less than 30 or 40 people

In more detail:

Brainstorming. Peter Drucker touches upon this in his book *Innovation and Entrepreneurship*. Especially as a company becomes larger, there is a risk of ossifying into rigid habits. Drucker emphasizes that it must become a regular discipline to assemble the best engineers, sales people, product people, and managers, and have them talk freely and improvisationally about how to take advantage of the opportunities they see in front of them. Such sessions are the rare situation where you want everyone to talk, without requiring them to defend their ideas. Careful analysis comes later; the creative moment should be unhindered by the demand for data and research. You want as much diversity of opinion as possible. In this scenario, a group meeting functions well because the goal isn't productivity, but rather, maximizing the number of ideas generated. (As such, be wary if the conversation drifts to some seemingly urgent short-term subject.)

Keep in mind, there are some people who will never speak up at a large group meeting, no matter how much you tell them *all* ideas are welcome. Some people are introverts or prefer to write out their ideas over oral communication. Make sure to include other communication options for those individuals before or after a large brainstorming meeting so you don't miss out on good ideas from those employees.

In another scenario, when you simply want to get a lot of information, perhaps from people with different experiences, a big group meeting is useful. For instance, if I'm trying to figure out a new architecture for a company, I'll informally poll my most experienced tech friends, asking them what database or message queue they would recommend for the situation I'm facing. Occasionally, I'll treat everyone to lunch, in exchange for their ideas. In such situations, the goal is not efficient use of time, but rather, to uncover a wide range of ideas.

In a similar vein, post-mortems, after some disaster, should kick off with a brainstorming session. Every team that might have insights about the disaster should be invited to share ideas about why things went badly. Once a large number of possibilities have been nominated, one person should be appointed to go off and investigate the matter in detail, calling in help as they need it.

Big wins should be celebrated. Hitting an ambitious sales goal or closing a round of funding are both good examples of reasons to have a party for your team or company (depending on the size of the company). At a social event, productivity is not the point. It's a moment to feel part of a group, perhaps a moment to spark a collective identity. Rituals, ceremonies, awards, and giving recognition to outstanding individuals — these things help everyone avoid burnout, by reminding them that work is a place of human connections.

Cross-functional teams can be highly effective. They have been a part of big corporate culture for more than 30 years now. Instead of a lone engineer coming up with an idea, then trying to convince finance to make a budget for it, then trying to convince marketing they can sell it, then trying to convince the design team to prioritize it — a process that famously took months or years at the big corporations of the mid-20th Century — a cross-functional team can mean each function is represented by one person on a small team, and together they can make fast decisions, outside of the normal rules of the larger bureaucracy. But since cross-functional teams mostly make sense at giant corporations with giant bureaucracies, they are outside of the scope of this book, which is focused on small- and medium-sized businesses.

Additionally, in large organizations, asking a person to give a presentation to a large group can be a way of promoting that person, while also indicating to the entire organization that the person has your full support. Whether in academia, the military, government, or business, it's a kind of promotion when you ask someone to give a talk to a room full of people. But those kinds of large-scale organizational politics are also beyond the scope of this book.

Extroverts like to talk. In business you often have to accommodate the actual strengths and weaknesses of a team. Sometimes you'll have a team where people prefer talking rather than writing, so they'd prefer a big meeting rather than making announcements via email or Slack or WhatsApp. I've seen this especially with sales teams, as such teams often attract extroverts.

However, accommodation has to go both ways. Even with sales, I've rarely seen a team so homogeneous that every person on the team feels the same way about meetings. Even in a room full of extroverts, you will typically find a few introverts.

The all-hands rally. I've seen a lot of startups that have a once-a-week all-hands meeting. This huge meeting is exactly as unproductive and inefficient as you might expect, but it is very useful as a morale boosting event. The early days of any startup tend to be exhausting and it is easy for people to get burned out, so having a once-a-week rally to celebrate the small wins of each week is important. At some point these meetings get to be too big, but for startups that have less than 30 or 40 people, these once-a-week meetings are a good idea.

French managers don't have meetings, they have dinner

There's an old joke that French managers don't have meetings, they have dinner. American managers would be wise to import this social convention. I've seen the occasional sales team go out for drinks, and sometimes when the tech or marketing team works late, they go out to celebrate. Social events are moments to turn away from work and focus on the human aspects of one's professional life.

Whenever I'm leading a tech team, I invite members to lunch as often as possible. Productivity isn't the goal, so a bigger group can be invited. This is especially important when someone is new to the team — I want to make them feel welcome, so inviting them to join a few of us for lunch is a great way to get to know them, away from the pressures of a specific agenda.

You've probably heard the saying "People don't quit jobs, they quit managers." Take your team to lunch and get to know them as people. Then you won't be one of the managers that they want to quit.

Having lunch or dinner with your team can blur the line between one's work and one's personal life. Sometimes this is a negative thing, and sometimes it's positive. On the positive side, your spouse or significant other is typically interested in what your work is like, and such after-hour social events are a moment when they can join you and meet the people you work with.

Fundamentally, humans work, work is human, humans are social, and so all work is social. Having lunch or dinner together is a chance to focus on each other as humans rather than workers. At such social gatherings, I've forged many friendships that long outlasted our temporary allegiance to any particular employer. Indeed, a successful career is often based around those friendships rather than any particular company. At the same time, I've found that building those friendships allowed me to enjoy a particular job much more than I would have otherwise, and every worker who works with you will probably feel the same.

Put differently: social events are not group meetings. There is no agenda, no goal, no urgency, and no need for productivity. That's why they are the perfect time to assemble a group that is much larger than what you would gather if you were actually worried about a goal or productivity.

Chapter 3

Shouting at a room is idiotic

Some leaders have suggested to me that big meetings are necessary for enforcing a kind of discipline. If things are going badly, if workers are lazy, why not call them all together and chastise them as a group for being lazy? Perhaps threaten them? Tell them they suck and they all need to do better?

In truth, this is never justified. A bad apple should be removed from the barrel, but you don't throw away the good apples in the barrel. In most situations, people are working hard. If there is a bad worker, they are an exception and not the rule, so you should sit down with them, alone, and tell them what they need to do to improve. If they are unable to improve, then they should be fired. If you honestly have a situation where every single worker is terrible, then fire yourself, because you have done a terrible job of hiring.

Ah, but what if you are taking over the job from a previous manager who was terrible? You then have no way of knowing who is good and who is bad, and the best way to find out is a series of one-on-one meetings. You don't learn anything by shouting at a room. This style of leadership suggests a leader for whom the workers are as interchangeable as ants, and people who are treated as ants will focus their energy on avoiding being stepped on; they won't focus their energy on doing a good job.

Self-control is essential to pragmatic leadership

Consider the following, which I see as an example of terrible leadership:

> Better.com CEO Vishal Garg publicly accused hundreds of staffers he laid off on Wednesday of "stealing" from their colleagues and customers by being unproductive.

(A year earlier, he had sent this mass email):

> You are TOO DAMN SLOW. You are a bunch of DUMB DOLPHINS and...DUMB DOLPHINS get caught in nets and eaten by sharks. SO STOP IT. STOP IT. STOP IT RIGHT NOW. YOU ARE EMBARRASSING ME.

> https://fortune.com/2021/12/03/
> better-com-ceo-attacks-laid-off-employees-blind-message-board/

As both George Orwell and Margaret Thatcher have emphasized, incorrect metaphors tend to suggest muddy thinking. In the real world, dolphins are as likely to eat sharks as vice versa. A good metaphor suggests a vivid image that's true to people's experiences, so "You are a bunch of dumb dolphins" fails on multiple levels.

Also, that last part, "you are embarrassing me," suggests an element of narcissism. It personalizes the feedback, something every leader should avoid doing. Whatever the problem is, the fact that the CEO feels embarrassed should be the least concern of anyone. The Board can always fire the CEO. What matters, in the long run, is whether the company is doing well. If the CEO is truly embarrassed, they should resign their position and allow the Board to appoint someone better.

Also, the use of all-caps is commonly thought of as a kind of written shouting, which indicates a lack of emotional control. That's something a good leader, on rare occasions, may pretend to do strategically — but no good leader ever does it accidentally. This email's lack of emotional control seems accidental.

Good feedback is specific and individual:

- If a worker has made a good-faith effort and failed, angry ranting doesn't help the worker. If they were going as fast as possible, but it wasn't fast enough, then you'll need to teach them how to do it faster. You don't need to be angry to do that, you only need to be forthright and direct and specific.
- If the worker has been operating in bad faith, then when you shout at everyone, you've encouraged them to continue, because you've made clear that you cannot tell the good workers from the bad workers. If you knew who the bad workers were, you would talk to them one-on-one, or perhaps fire them. But apparently you can't tell the difference, so the bad-faith workers now know they can continue to operate in bad faith, because you're unable to see them for what they are. Calm, quiet conversations with specific workers will reveal to you who is good and who is bad.

Sometimes when I say this to my clients, they respond with some variation of, "Yeah, it would be great if we were all Zen Buddhists, but I've got to be pragmatic, I've got to run a business."

I'd like to point out that self-control *is* in fact pragmatic. And shouting at a whole room full of people is not.

Less than a year after sending the above email, Vishal Garg laid off 900 employees, roughly 15% of the company. Apparently screaming that they were dumb dolphins failed to improve their productivity.

Especially when you have to deliver bad news to your workers, your own self-control matters. You need to offer your empathy to them; you should not be demanding that they be empathetic to you. As an example, saying that you have cried or that you feel like crying can be seen as a manipulative attempt to gain sympathy for oneself. When he announced the mass layoffs, Garg said:

> This is the second time in my career that I'm doing this and I do not want to do this. The last time I did it I cried. This time I hope to be stronger. But we are laying off about 15% of the company for [a number of] reasons: the market, efficiency and performances and productivity.

https://www.bbc.com/news/business-59554585

The remaining 85% of the company must now move forward knowing they have a leader who, when announcing mass layoffs, wants the workers to feel sympathy for him. This cannot be good for morale.

"You are embarrassing me!"

Besides sounding a like a 13 year-old asking their mom to leave the room so they can be alone with their friends, the phrase "You are embarrassing me" suggests several even deeper problems:

1. The company originates mortgages and expanded aggressively during the early part of the Covid-19 pandemic, when the real estate market was red hot. Having raised $900 million, they briefly felt they had money to burn. When the market cooled in 2021, they were overstaffed. In other words, the culpability

for layoffs probably lies with the aggressive expansion overseen by the CEO. It's unlikely that the workers are to blame.

2. Of the mass layoffs, Vishal Garg said, "This is the second time in my career I've had to do this," suggesting he has a habit of aggressive over-expansion.

3. When dealing with restructurings or layoffs, the most important task involves taking responsibility for mistakes. Even assuming that the workers were terrible, who hired them? Garg was both a founder and the only CEO of the five year-old company. Every single person at the company was either hired by Garg or hired by a manager who was hired by Garg. If Garg routinely hires bad workers, or if he hires bad managers who then hire bad workers, then Garg is a poor leader. He needs to improve several of his skills, including how to listen to feedback, how to give feedback, how to delegate authority, and how to hire.

4. Why is Garg talking to every employee? Why aren't their managers delivering the message? Be careful when you decide to break out of the hierarchy that you created at your company. I admit, there is no absolute right or wrong answer here — I've known great managers who sometimes break out of the hierarchy and I've known terrible managers who were careful not to break out of the hierarchy. But most of the time, if a worker needs to improve, that message should come from their manager, not from the CEO. Especially in a large company, the CEO cannot possibly know each worker, so any feedback coming from the CEO is going to be vague and non-actionable — "Don't be a dumb dolphin" instead of something specific, such as, "You only made 20 cold calls last week, but I expect you to make 25."

(Just as I wrote these words, it was announced that the Board was removing Garg from his position.)

When does the whole company need to hear from the CEO?

Some well-known and successful CEOs insist that they must frequently speak to the whole company, perhaps through a mass rally or a video address. This is a subtle issue, with interesting arguments on both sides. Typically, such CEOs suggest that people do not read email, therefore email is a bad way to disperse a detailed strategic idea. Such CEOs also implicitly distrust their direct reports to spread such a message, indeed, some of these CEOs have explicitly said that relying on direct reports to disperse an idea leads to a giant game of telephone: the message gets increasingly distorted the further it travels. But how important is it that such messages come from the CEO? This question dovetails with the question of whether a large organization should be made legible to the person at the top. How you feel about that question is how you will feel about this kind of communication. Does a mass rally really offer a good moment for communication of a detailed strategic idea? I'd suggest that these rallies are mostly used to spread a marketing message, and in fact, when these mass rallies function well, they function mostly as morale-boosting events; which strikes me as a perfectly reasonable thing to do, so long as one doesn't do it too often.

Chapter 4

Skip level one-on-ones. Who should you talk to?

Should you ever meet with someone who reports to someone who reports to you? This is the so-called "skip level one-on-one." The terminology is relatively new, but the idea is old.

If you're the CEO, it's often useful to talk to people throughout the organization, no matter what your relationship is with them. David Packard, in his book, *The HP Way: How Bill Hewlett and I Built Our Company*, talked about the informal style they developed at Hewlett Packard in the 1940s and 1950s. Walking down a hallway, Hewlett might bump into some engineer, and he'd ask, hey, what are you working on? And then the engineer would explain their project, so Hewlett got to hear some interesting details that he would never hear from a corporate memo. Hewlett and Packard jokingly referred to this as MBWA (Management By Walking Around). This can be thought of as a type of skip level one-on-one, conversations with people deep in the organization. Keep in mind, this is wonderful so long as the goal is information gathering — but if the engineer had a problem and Hewlett interrupted his day to deal with the problem, then the question would come up, why was the manager of that engineer unable to solve the problem? One benefit of MBWA is that occasionally the top leadership discovers they have a weak manager who isn't solving problems for their team. However, the lesson from this should be "replace weak managers with excellent managers," not "the top leadership needs to solve everyone's problems."

Almost any new manager, in a new role, can benefit from skip level one-on-ones. The following is from Jason Wong:

> When I was promoted to Engineering Director, I had no idea what I was doing. It was a role that I had little to no prior experience with, and it took me the better part of 18 months to figure out how to be effective in it. I characterize my performance during that time as being just useful enough to not get fired.
>
> As it turned out, skip-level one-on-ones became an invaluable tool— one of the things that I feel like I actually got right during my tenure as a senior leader. Among the many benefits, skip-level one-on-ones helped me build a stronger relationship with my organization, understand of [sic] how my managers were performing, and gain first hand accounts of how my decisions were affecting the people in my organization ...
>
> One of the primary rules to abide by in skip level one-on-ones is do not preempt your manager. The ability to affect outcomes through your managers is a difficult and vital skill to learn as a senior leader. Skip-level one-on-ones will definitely test your discipline in this regard. If engineers learn they can short-circuit their manager by taking their issues directly to you, that's a breeding ground for terribleness for everyone involved. If you find yourself compelled to do something, be very clear with that person about what level of involvement they should expect from you.
>
> https://jwongworks.com/blog/2019/4/16/the-skip-level-1-1

In particular, if a manager is hired from outside the company and now needs to learn about the division they've been asked to manage, skip level one-on-ones offer a powerful education for the new manager. However, if such skip level meetings become habitual and feel crucial to maintaining the health of the organization, then you have to ask yourself, why do the top leaders/ managers need to so often break out of the hierarchy of the organization? One possibility is that some of your lower level managers are weak, but another possibility is that your organization is too hierarchical. If you find that you often need to talk to the direct report of a direct report, then *why* are they the direct report of a direct report? Maybe they should report to you?

Especially problematic is if you find yourself talking to all of the reports of a report, that is, everyone who works for someone who reports to you – which almost always means that you're micromanaging the situation. If you change your behavior and cold-turkey quit this habit, does anything bad happen? If not, then you were definitely micromanaging. If things do fall apart without your direct attention, then your direct report is incompetent and it's therefore falling upon you to manage their team. Find someone better.

I recently spoke with Eric Garside, who has been head of technology at Freshly for five years and who grew the tech team from four people to 70 people. At one point he had 15 direct reports, which strikes me as a high number, but it gave him deep insight into what the team was doing. Even when there were 30 engineers on the team, none were more than one level away from him. This was during a time when he himself was still close to the technology and even sometimes contributing code.

Of course, things change. As Freshly matured, Garside found himself spending more time interacting with the other top level leaders — the head of marketing, the head of operations, etc. As such, he could no longer spend as much time managing the details of the tech team. At that point, he divided the tech team into two main divisions, and he took the two team leads that he trusted most and put them in charge of those two divisions. In other words, he went from having 15 direct reports to having only two. Having 15 direct reports granted him insight into fine-grained details about the operations of the tech team but it also took too much of his time. He was looking down the hierarchy, but at a certain point he needed to look up. Trusting the tech team to his two lieutenants freed him to spend more time interacting with the rest of the company. This approach worked well for him and for Freshly.

The needs of an organization will always change over time, and therefore your role as a leader will change too. Even the CEO faces the question of when they should focus down the hierarchy and when they should focus up — for the CEO, facing up the hierarchy typically means focusing on the investors and the Board of Directors. I wish there was an easy-to-follow formula that would magically achieve the ideal balance, but in fact this is something that can only be understood through trial and error. Discovering the right level of hierarchy for your organization is an art, not a science, and it is something that needs to be constantly rediscovered as the situation changes. Sometimes you will need less hierarchy and sometimes you will need more, but the only way to know is to keep track of the real needs of your team and to balance those needs against the needs of all the other teams in the company.

Should a high-level manager focus on their peers, or on those whom they lead?

There is no right answer to this question, but I'd like to share some patterns I've observed.

Picture a new startup which hires a talented developer to create the software. The whole startup consists of just four people, including the CEO, the marketing person, the content person, and the software developer. Everything is going great, and soon the startup triples in size. Now the software developer is the team lead, with two software developers reporting to them. The team leader's job is still mostly technical, the managerial burden is light, and all three developers spend their time writing code. But then the startup triples in size again, and then again.

Now the tech team has 27 people in it. That original developer is given the title of Chief Technology Officer. The tech team breaks up into seven smaller teams: the frontend of the public site, the frontend of their internal dashboard, the business intelligence dashboards, the database, the devops, the iPhone team, and the Android team. The CTO still thinks of their job as being mostly technical and wants to closely monitor the developments on each team, so the leader of each team reports to the CTO and they have frequent meetings. The CTO might even occasionally check out the actual code bases, run it on their personal machine, examine the quality of the code, perhaps write some code and submit a pull request. The engineers love having a leader who understands them so well.

This CTO is loved by the software developers but disliked by their peers. The CMO feels unheard, the CFO thinks the CTO doesn't show enough concern for the budget, the Chief Content Officer (CCO) feels that their team is crippled because the CTO doesn't understand their publishing needs. Such moments can undermine the career of a CTO. I'm aware of at least one case where, ten years after the situation arose, the CMO and CFO and COO, who had all moved on to new jobs at new companies, were still whispering rumors about the CTO. When the CTO applied for a new job, and the company asked his former peers what they thought of him, they were told, "He is uncooperative, he is not a team player." So clearly, in that case, it would have been better for the CTO if he'd spent less time with his tech team and more time with his C-level peers. Or rather, there must have been some particular moment in the growth of the company when it would have been best for the CTO to switch his focus away from tech and towards his peers, but the CTO missed that moment, much to the irritation of his peers.

Another pattern I've seen is the talented computer science student who does brilliantly in college, developing some interesting software, or maybe goes straight from undergrad to graduate school. They start their career in their mid-20s, and because they have some advanced degree or project, they skip over the long years in the trenches working as a regular computer programmer. Their first job is often as CTO of a startup, or at a high-level in a medium-sized company, or, as we saw at Twitter, AirBnB, and Parsely, the CTO of a startup that is quickly funded and so instantly becomes huge. Often such CTOs find it natural to talk to their C-level peers, to understand the needs of each team in the company, and to think strategically about what the company might need overall. Most eventually leave tech behind and become head of product, or chief of strategy. Indeed, meeting with other C-level leaders and talking in abstract terms about the future resembles what they did in countless school exercises, so this activity is a comfortable one for them. But they are fairly incompetent at the basic task of understanding the worries of the software developers who work for them. Having never worked professionally as a software developer, they have no affinity for the work; they lack any understanding of its natural cadence. (This is not a fatal flaw, but such CTOs need to know their weaknesses and adjust to them by finding a good project manager, someone who does understand the cadence of tech work. The CTO then needs to defer to the time estimates generated by that project manager. There might be many areas where such a CTO needs to find expert help, and defer to it.)

You might be wondering if I've ever seen anyone get it exactly right, the perfect balance between focusing on one's own team versus focusing on the needs of the other teams in the company. My answer would be, "Yes, for a while." The situation is fluid and changes from month to month, so there is no perfect balance that lasts.

What would the Roman Emperor Hadrian do?

During the era of the Roman Empire, there was a tradition that people could wait in the Forum, and when the Emperor came through, they would be allowed to petition for redress of their grievances. One day, in 121 AD, the Roman Emperor Hadrian was walking through the Forum, concerned with some emergency that was demanding his attention. An old woman, who had been waiting for several days to speak with him, started to explain her situation, but he shouted, "I have no time! I have no time!"

To which the old woman responded, "Then rule no more!"

Supposedly, the Emperor Hadrian took this to heart. He realized he must find the time to listen, if he were to rule well.

Hadrian is remembered as one of the great reformers, passing important laws that made life better for the people of the empire. Historians agree, the excellence of his leadership owes a lot to the fact that he traveled around and listened to the people who were affected by his governance.

So, too, the very small empire that you will be running. Everyone in a leadership position should remember: you must find the time to listen, if you are going to rule well.

Specifically, there is one kind of skip level one-on-one that you always need to be ready to accept. As your organization gets larger, there is the risk that someone will be disrespectful (or even abusive) to others in the organization. This issue can be handled by your managers, unless the problem is one of the managers themselves. While you shouldn't feel the need to answer for every problem in your organization, you do need to answer for the actions of your managers. For the sake of fairness, as well as the long-term health of your organization, everyone has to know that they can bring you their problems — at least when their manager is the problem.

Please, please, please: learn how to walk before you try to run a marathon

Imagine a man in his thirties who is addicted to video

games. He plays them all day long. Out of shape, he finds himself short of breath every time he walks up a flight of steps. Then something happens, perhaps a health crisis or the death of a loved one, which makes him see his life differently. He decides he needs to change. There are many programs that could help guide him as he slowly rebuilds his muscles, tendons, cartilage and cardiovascular system. For instance, *Couch to 5K* is a good program. Simply going for a long walk each day would be a solid program for someone badly out of shape. But instead of doing the slow work of building up to a 5k run, he starts reading about ultra-marathons. Awestruck, he memorizes facts about those who can run for 50 miles or more. Famous incidents, terrible accidents, unusual weather, upset wins — he memorizes it all. None of which helps him get back into shape. In fact, this focus on ultra-marathons is, if anything, a distraction from the real work he should be doing. Barely able to walk a mile, he daydreams about running for 50.

I'm sad to say that I've worked with entrepreneurs who preside over badly run, poorly performing organizations, but who fantasize about incorporating the advanced disciplines of the U.S. military. Rather than admiring these entrepreneurs for their ambition, I've learned to doubt them because of their distance from reality.

There is an abundance of business books that promote elite performance as if it were the norm by which we should measure ourselves. Here are two of them:

1. *Extreme Ownership: How U.S. Navy SEALs Lead and Win*, by Jocko Willink and Leif Babin.

2. *Semper Fi: Business Leadership the Marine Corps Way*, by Dan Carrison and Rod Walsh.

To be clear, many of these books are very good. My concern is that some of them amount to the fantasy of running an ultra-marathon when a person is a couch potato who can barely get out the front door.

I'll provide a quote from one of my favorites. In their book *The Discipline of Teams,* Jon R. Katzenback and Douglas K. Smith write:

The most important characteristic of teams is discipline; not bonding, togetherness, or empowerment. Perhaps the finest examples of small group performance are in the U.S. Marine Corps (USMC). Some of the small groups qualify as teams and some do not. But whatever small group configuration is required, the USMC invariably uses the right one at the right time. The reason is discipline. Discipline is a three-dimensional concept for the USMC. Top-down command and control is alive and well, but it is no match for the peer discipline and self-discipline that create value-driven Marines.

It is this three-dimensional discipline that ensures that the leadership role in a USMC fire team will shift, depending on who has the high ground. This same discipline motivates rifle platoon leadership teams, where a gunnery sergeant might tell his captain to change the intended tactical maneuver because he, the gunny, perceives a better way.

It is this discipline that motivates every rifleman to act on the intent of leaders two levels up, since intent always takes precedence over any direct command to the contrary. Moreover, the USMC can apply real-team discipline with the same conviction and facility as they apply the single leader discipline, for which they are better known. Marines are masters of team performance because they are proficient at not one, but two disciplines that create versatile, powerful performance units.

It is not happenstance that this book is titled *The Discipline of Teams*, the sequel and companion to our earlier work, *The Wisdom of Teams*. In fact, for the first book, we might have easily chosen discipline for the title instead of wisdom, since we certainly recognized its importance at the time. We even called our definition of teams a discipline. What we failed to appreciate fully, however,

is the difficulty many would encounter in differentiating and inte-
grating the team and single-leader disciplines. That difficulty, more
than anything else, warrants this sequel, which we sincerely hope
will provide additional help to the readers of and believers in *The
Wisdom of Teams* as they work hard to get real teams in the right
places at the right times for the right reasons.

... Understanding the value and potential of teams has proved to
be much easier than applying the discipline required in achieving
team performance.

(To be clear, when they speak of "teams" they do not just
mean "groups." Rather, they refer to situations where an entire
group, rather than an individual leader, takes responsibility for
meeting a goal.)

Much can be learned from these books, but I also urge caution. A person who joins the Marines is a person who is ready
to die for their country. By contrast, the frontend designer who
agrees to take your Photoshop or Figma design and turn it into
working code is just a civilian who wants to do their job and then
go home to their family. They have not agreed to die for you.

While these books offer a fascinating look at high-perform-
ing organizations, some of the behavior patterns described take
years of training to develop, for both the leaders and the led.
Merely reading a book, and then trying to implement the ideas,
might lead to chaotic results. Don't underestimate how hard it
can be to replicate the performance culture of the U.S. Marines.

If you happen to oversee a well-run organization, and you
want to take performance up to an even higher level, then these
books can offer useful insights about the kind of disciplines you
and your staff need to develop. But again, many of the places that I have worked at or consulted with have been far from
ideal, and I urge them to learn the basics before trying something advanced. Don't assume you're ready to storm the beaches
of Normandy when you and your employees have not yet grad-
uated from basic training.

The most basic of all management techniques is developing rapport with one other person by having good one-on-one conversations. Get that right before you start dreaming of the management equivalent of an ultra-marathon.

Chapter 5

One-on-one conversations are a cure for passive-aggressive text

In recent years, I have worked as a high level tech consultant. As my hourly rate goes higher and higher, I face more pressure to prove that I can make positive changes, fast. This has caused a revolution in my approach to learning about an organization.

Back when I was simply a software developer, I would join an organization, accept whatever task I was given, and write the necessary code. I assumed I would slowly learn about the overall organization, in a process of osmosis, given time. If you've read my book *How To Destroy A Tech Startup In Three Easy Steps* then you've already seen my old style: focused on coding, and merely an observer of the chaos around me. But my role has changed dramatically over the last seven years. Being a high level consultant means I have to come up to speed in a week or two. Toward this end, I've developed a much more direct, aggressive approach towards learning, and this process relies on asking for a one-on-one meeting with anyone in an organization who might be able to teach me something about the problems that the organization is facing.

In 2019, I was asked to help a company I'll call OxyMetaFin, a fast growing startup that offered financial services to those who only had very small amounts of money to invest. Having opened up the world of investing to a demographic that had been previously excluded, this startup enjoyed explosive growth. Their tech stack was built with the Ruby On Rails framework. However, they had made some tragically poor technical decisions, which threatened to derail their growth.

What were the real problems? How did they manifest? Who did they affect? I needed to learn all of this fast. So I set up one-on-one meetings with:

- the CEO
- the other C-levels – Chief of Operations (COO), Finance (CFO), Marketing (CMO), and Products (CPO)
- the lead graphic designer, who reported to the CPO
- the head of customer service
- the head of the business intelligence team
- the woman who oversaw the team in Brazil that handled most customer complaints
- the gentleman in Brazil who oversaw the team locally (he was the owner of that company)
- the various liaisons to our stock market information sources, traders, and international traders (all 3rd party)
- the project manager who helped keep the tech team organized (this woman seemed better informed than anyone else about every aspect of the company, and I came to rely on her to the point that I spoke with her almost every day)

So, for the first two weeks almost all I did was engage in one-on-one conversations, doing a deep dive into the problems of the company.

What I learned was that the company had, in the early days, setup a database, poorly tuned it, felt it was overwhelmed, then set up another database to store a subset of the data (time series data in a database optimized for time series), then they set up another database to power the frontend (a document store storing JSON), then they set up a cache, and then they started storing canonical data in every one of these different data stores. In short, there was no canonical source of truth in the company, but instead, every data store was a sad mix of cache and truth. A total nightmare from the perspective of clean software development.

During the third week I came up with a tentative plan for unifying the sources of data. During the fourth week I worked with the software developers to work out the specifics of what changes in the code would be necessary, and then what chronological order we should follow to implement the new plan.

Over the next few months, great progress was made to improve the centralization of data, and the ways it was accessed, and this in turn helped smooth operations for everyone else, including the customers, and also customer service (who got less and less angry complaints from customers, as the software improved).

But let's back up a bit. Towards the end of the second week is when I started having odd interactions with a programmer named Pei, a programmer who had been at the company for four years and who therefore had been there longer than any other member of the tech team. This was a text exchange on Slack:

Me: Hi, Pei. I haven't yet had a chance to talk to you one-on-one. You are the most experienced software developer at this company, so I'm eager to hear your ideas about how the company should move forward. What are the biggest problems? What are the biggest opportunities? Can we schedule some time to talk?

Pei: Hey, welcome. I'm glad you signed up. We have some fun stuff ahead. I'll have to get back to you on meetings.

Me: Thank you. I'm excited to be here. My schedule is fairly flexible, so just let me know a time that's available on your side, and we can put it on the calendar.

Pei: Sure. You should focus on learning about the company. Your first few weeks, you'll need to learn a lot.

Me: Absolutely. I want to learn as much as possible as fast as possible. That's why I'd like to talk to you, whenever you have some time.

Pei: Yeah, we'll be working together a lot. I can answer all of your questions.

Me: Yes, I was told you've been here longer than any other computer programmer?

Pei: Yes, four years. Nobody else was able to last that long.

Me: Great, so you understand where everything is and how it all ties together?

Pei: Yes, but I've rebuilt everything. Going forward the team will use my new version of the code. I put everything in Docker to speed future development.

Me: Awesome. Great job. I'd love to learn more about that, if you have any time in your schedule.

Pei: I don't have much time to talk. I'm facing hard deadlines. Massive hard deadlines. They keep piling more and more onto me.

What to make of this? Was he asking for pity? He seemed to have a lot of time to chat on Slack, but for some reason he didn't want to talk to me directly over video.

Me: I realize you are very busy.

Pei: There are 11 main repos. I'm sending you some info on how they tie together. I wrote a bash script that will do the work for you. Just run the bash script.

Me: Fantastic. This will help me get things running on my laptop.

Pei: That is the goal, yes.

Me: So, you've made it easier for new software developers to get going?

Pei: Yes, that is what I do. I join an organization, I figure out what it needs, I analyze the situation carefully, and then I do the actual work that makes life easier for everyone else. When I'm allowed to, I save organizations from chaos. My brain is designed for the meta layer of problems, the systemic problems. I see the big picture, and I fix problems at the scale of that big picture.

Was that true? If the code was a mess, and he was the longest serving member of the tech team, then shouldn't he take some of the blame for the code being a mess? What did he mean when he said "when I'm allowed to?" Was he trying to say that someone had stopped him from fixing the problems in the code? Was he being defensive?

Me: Fantastic. As soon as you have time, I'd love to dive into the details.

Pei: It will take you months to learn the details.

Me: Well, I'll learn as fast as I can.

Pei: You don't have to do everything on your own, thankfully. My role right now is kind of mixing into yours, but along with expectations of full development, so my time is much more limited than yours. I would just take a deep breath and give it a few weeks. You're already way ahead of where I was when I started, because I've done so much work to clean things up for you.

Me: I'm sure the team is grateful that you've managed to bring order out of chaos.

Pei: How well do you know Ruby On Rails? There is a kind of Zen to Ruby. Some people get it and some people don't. Let's plan at some point some practice sessions to make sure you are up to speed. If you plan major architectural achievements that require us to work together, you'll find Rails will be a good playground for that. I'll make sure your skills are current and you are able to work in Rails.

Wow. What was I supposed to do with that? My technical skills had already been vetted by the CTO, there was no reason for Pei to arrogate this responsibility to himself. He and I were both highly experienced engineers – he had about 15 years of experience, and I had 20. If he wanted to challenge my credentials, I wanted to have that conversation face to face over video, not merely in text on Slack.

Me: The CTO reviewed my previous work before I started here, but of course, when I have code to push, I'm sure you'll be part of the code review process. I look forward to whatever comments you might have at that time.

Silence. An hour went by and he didn't write anything. It is possible that he was called into another meeting, or he had some other work to do, or maybe he was trying to snub me. One problem with communication over Slack, versus talking to someone in an office, is that there are more ways for miscommunication to develop. And then:

> Pei: Ok, I think what you need to do is gather up your most important questions and go after those goals first. You need to prioritize. You won't be able to do everything, so you're going to have to figure out what the most urgent issues are. If you try to do everything at once, you're simply going to fail.

> Me: You are right, we need to prioritize. I'd like to get your input. That's why I'd like to schedule a one-on-one meeting.

> Pei: Just so long as you understand, this won't be easy. I'm worried you think this is easy. The code is complex. There is no simple fix. This is going to take real work. So think about what your top priority is. You need to get that right, or you will fail.

Why was he telling me how to do my job? Before I'd even started, I wrote a 10 page Word document full of standard questions that I use to orient myself quickly at a new company. My questions roughly follow what Amazon now refers to as the "AWS Well-Architected framework." Like the framework, my questions revolve around six pillars: operational excellence, security, reliability, performance efficiency, cost optimization, and sustainability. I'd already discussed this with the CTO and we'd agreed that operational excellence and reliability were the two points of real crisis.

Was Pei jealous? Perhaps he felt that he should have been given the role of coming up with a rescue plan? That would be interesting to talk about, directly, during our one-on-one meeting. I did not want to have such a conversation through a series of sniping remarks on Slack.

I reviewed Pei's resume and I spoke to the project manager about him. Here is what I learned: he has 15 years experience, all of it as a Ruby On Rails engineer. He has no management experience. He has no substantial experience with other programming languages. He has no experience with infrastructure (devops). From this I concluded: when it comes to Ruby on Rails he is far more talented than I will ever be. I'm a generalist who has done professional work in eight different languages, plus I've done substantial infrastructure (devops) work, plus I have substantial management experience. He is a specialist who knows Rails deeply. (As it turned out, when I eventually pushed some Rails code, he did the code review, and I learned a lot from his feedback.)

A good argument can be made for Pei, and he is the person who should make that argument. But he shouldn't be making it to me. He should have made it to the CTO. Before I was ever called in, Pei could have asked for a one-on-one meeting with the CTO and then said: "I am a great engineer, and it is time for me to begin to gain management experience. I'd like to be given the role of overseeing the revamp of our overall system. We don't need to bring in an outside consultant, just give the whole job to me." And then the CTO would have said yes or no. If yes, then great, Pei has the job of his dreams. If no, okay, then Pei has to decide if he can live with that decision, or whether he should quit and find a place that sees his potential the same way he sees it. Either way, direct, honest, one-on-one communication with the CTO is going to give him clarity about his potential and his future. Sniping at me in Slack does nothing. It's stupid, but worse than that, it is ineffective.

Still, he couldn't avoid me forever. The next week I finally got him to agree to a one-on-one conversation, via video. And when we finally spoke that way, I was surprised by how meek he was.

Me: So, I see two issues as being central. One, the data. We need to have a clear source of truth. And the other big issue is monitoring, broadly defined. We are currently flying blind. The engineers have some intuition about what is working and what is broken, but we don't have many facts.

Pei: Yes, I agree.

Me: We don't know which database queries are slow. We don't know which parts of the code generate the most bugs. We don't know how often API calls to 3rd parties fail. We have no integration tests, no health checks, no log analysis.

Pei: I agree, this is important.

Me: So I'm thinking we need to get more monitoring in place, more unit tests, more integration tests, more real-time health checks.

Pei: Yes, I agree.

Me: Towards that end, we also need to put in place a CI/CD system, from where we can run the tests. Also, it will give us more flexibility in setting up test environments for the development team.

Pei: Yes, that is true.

Me: If we start using Docker in production, the CI/CD tool can also do that for us.

Pei: Yes. Can I also suggest setting up our infrastructure to run Kubernetes?

Me: We wouldn't ever run Kubernetes ourselves.

Pei: Why? We could get security, scalability, isolation, everything we need, if we commit to the combination of Docker and Kubernetes.

Me: We won't ever run Kubernetes ourselves. We might run Docker on AWS Fargate, which I think uses Kubernetes under the hood. But we can rely on some other service to do that for us. We won't do it ourselves, we don't have the time or resources to deal with that extra layer of complexity.

Pei: I feel like you haven't really thought about this.

Me: I have thought about this and I have discussed this with the CTO and my final decision is that we can rely on other services to run our Dockerized apps. We don't need to run Kubernetes ourselves.

Pei: Um... okay.

Me: Are we agreed these are the priorities?

Pei: Sure. Let me know how I can help.

Me: I will. Thank you.

Pei: I'm just here to help.

Me: Thank you.

I have dealt with this personality type before: unable or unwilling to express their frustrations in a face to face conversation, their frustration instead leaks out in a series of oddly aggressive text messages, either in email or in a chat app like Slack. Going forward, I'd have to adjust my style with Pei, recognizing that what he truly felt would be expressed in weird text messages, and I'd just have to filter out the aggression and focus on whatever grain of truth remained. I'm happy to say, once we started having regular one-on-one conversations, the amount of weird aggression he expressed in text slowly decreased.

For anyone who is a bit like Pei, my recommendation is that

you force yourself to do more one-on-one conversations. This is especially true if you ever hope to move into management, but it's also true if you never want to go into management. Such conversations might force you to move beyond your comfort zone, but if you can get used to direct, honest, respectful communication in a one-on-one setting, you will become far more effective in your career, at whatever level you want to operate at. You don't need to shout, and you don't need to use curse words, you just have to be direct, straightforward, and honest. You should always be respectful, but realize there is no contradiction between being respectful and also being honest about someone's mistakes. So long as those mistakes are real, and you can talk about them honestly and without anger, then you should talk about them to prevent them from being repeated. Likewise, there is no contradiction between being respectful and setting a firm boundary (as I did with Pei, on the subject of Kubernetes).

Does this honesty run the risk that someone, sometime will think you are arrogant? Maybe, but it is better to come across as slightly arrogant, while setting a firm boundary, than to try to please people by saying things that you don't really mean. As an example, I had two alternatives regarding Pei (aside from being honest). I could let him think we would build our own Kubernetes infrastructure, only to tell him the truth a month later, at which point he could accurately accuse me of lying to him. Or I could simply give in and do what he wanted, risking my reputation and my career on a strategy that I thought was a mistake, all because I wanted to keep some random software developer happy. Do either of these options seem wise?

(Much of this advice about honest, direct communication also applies to romance.

I once had a friend who fell for a girl, and he invested enormous amounts of time into getting to know her, but without ever saying directly that he was pursuing a romance with her. And the girl, perhaps put off by the ambiguity of the situation, eventually put some limits on how much time she was willing to spend with him. Whereupon he complained to me that she had put him in the "friendzone." But it struck me that he had put himself there. Indeed, she had no power to put him there. The friendzone was a prison he designed for himself, and then chose to live in.

If you are interested in someone, then tell them. If they say "yes" then you can proceed. If they say "no" then you can walk away and forget about them. But if they say "no" and you then decide to waste the next year of your life pining after them, despite them rejecting you, then you've put yourself in the friendzone. No one has the power to put you there, except yourself.

I could write more, but I'll leave the further elaboration of how these ideas, about direct communication as it applies to romance, to some future book I might some day write.)

Chapter 6

Is anger ever justified? Is it ever strategic?

Okay, now we dive into a controversial topic. Some managers feel that they can use anger to get what they want at work. Some seem to use it strategically, and by that I mean, they pretend to be angry but they are not really angry. Rather, they use the act of being angry to provoke some reaction out of an employee.

I'm not talking about psychopaths. Studies show about 1% of all people are psychopaths, and these people end up being over-represented among managers. Most of us have some experience with these toxic bosses. However, psychopathic leaders are typically hated by their staff, and they often damage the organizations they work for, as the most talented staff will quit as quickly as they can. Here, though, I'm talking about something else: managers that create an overall positive environment, such that most of their workers really enjoy working with them. Yet these managers seem to believe that anger can be used to provoke honesty, or to provoke the manifestation of some other strategic goal.

Here is a true story about two men I've worked with several times over the course of several years. I'm going to call them Armsdale and Gary. This story was related to me by Gary. Keep in mind, most people really enjoy working for Armsdale, and that includes myself and Gary, but this story took place way back when Armsdale and Gary met for the first time.

Some years back a company I'll call Centauri was in trouble, and they called in a great devops engineer, Gary, to help them modernize their tech stack. They also brought in a great business consultant, Armsdale.

Armsdale perhaps thought that the new tech stack should be ready for use by March, but April arrived and the new tech stack still wasn't operational. So Armsdale called Gary into a meeting.

Armsdale: Have you set up the servers with the new Oracle databases?

Gary: Yes, the servers are running and the software is installed.

Armsdale: If that's true, what's the roadblock that keeps us from using this in production?

Gary: Mostly it's a matter of security. I don't know what roles or permissions we need in production.

Armsdale: That's what's blocking you? Who did you talk to about this?

Gary: I talked to the lead engineer, but they didn't know what roles or permissions would be needed on the business side.

Armsdale: So go talk to the business side. Do you realize we are running a month late?

Gary: My point of contact on the business side was Sally, the project manager, but she recently quit. I don't know who is going to replace her.

Armsdale (suddenly angry): Well, why don't you find out! Do you even care that we're running a month late?

Gary: I've spoken to Robin, who used to manage Sally, but she doesn't know either.

Armsdale: God damn it, someone has to know! Track it down! The databases are your job, and everything related to the databases! Do your damn job!

Gary: The problem is no one knows. Really no one. Not right now. The business intelligence team has planned some big changes, relative to the old system, but none of those changes have been finalized, so it's impossible to formalize their needs as a system of roles and permissions in the database.

Armsdale: And it never occurred to you to simply copy over the roles and permissions you were using in development? Are you a complete idiot?

Gary: Again, we weren't told what the new roles would be, so in development we left the database wide open to anyone.

Armsdale: Are you insane? Wide open to anyone? All the company secrets could be stolen!

Gary: No chance of that. I locked it down to the local network, so only engineers in the building could reach it. But for them, the database is wide open, they can do anything with it.

Armsdale: I'm tired of your excuses! It was your responsibility to set up the database and you've failed, and now we are a month late! If the lead engineer didn't know what the new roles and permissions would be, and if Robin didn't know, then you could have pressed them to press the business intelligence team to make some preliminary decisions! You could have done something to get your work back on schedule!

Gary (very calm): I did go talk to Robin. We had a long conversation about this. And she promised to put pressure on the business intelligence team. As a concession, they said they'd have at least a preliminary sketch of what they need by the end of business day tomorrow.

Armsdale (suddenly calm): Oh, I see. Okay, that's great. Well, move forward when you get their answer tomorrow. If you don't get what you need from them tomorrow, let me know and I'll put some pressure on them.

As unlikely as it seems, this was the start of a beautiful business relationship. Armsdale thereafter trusted Gary and called him in to a dozen different companies to help with a dozen different rescue missions.

Was Armsdale actually angry during this conversation? Probably not. He got angry with little provocation, and then a moment later his anger vanished without a trace. It's likely that he understood the strategic use of anger and in this case he was pretending to be angry so as to test Gary. Like some of the greatest managers, Armsdale is also a great actor, and can enact an imitation of anger whenever he needs to.

Those of you who have read my book *How To Destroy A Tech Startup In Three Easy Steps* will recall an even longer fight that I was involved in, with even more shouting on the part of my manager. In that case, one trick my manager pulled was when I didn't call him on the phone, he started to cry and demanded an apology from me, which I refused to offer. I wrote:

"He sounded like he was going to cry. This note of self-pity was surprising to me. My friends and I have sometimes discussed the right-wing television personality Glenn Beck and his tendency to cry on television. Is Beck truly overwhelmed with emotion as frequently as it seems, or is it all just an act? The best explanation I had ever heard, from a friend of mine who is a professional actress, was that a great actor fully experiences the emotions they're portraying — so it's possible that Beck is playing a character in one sense yet still genuinely feeling his emotional raptures in another. And I think something similar must be true of Milburn. On the one hand, it seems naive to think that he really felt such strong emotions over my failure to call him, but on the other hand, his emoting seemed entirely sincere."

Was this strategic? Keep in mind, I quit that company shortly after he pulled this fake crying stunt. So in that case his little stunt backfired on him. And yet, many otherwise talented managers do seem to feel that something like anger can be used strategically to get results.

In my experience, actual anger is never needed, nor is it a smart move. No one wants to work for a manager who is unable to control their emotions. Most of the managers who think they are being strategic in their use of manipulative tactics are in fact much more clumsy than they realize, so the tactics backfire more often than they work. Therefore, you should proceed with caution if this is a tactic you wish to employ.

More often than not, direct, honest, respectful communication is the right strategy: it gets people to do their jobs, do their jobs correctly, and do their jobs on time. Such communication establishes a culture of honesty, such that it becomes less likely that the workers will lie.

Are workers comfortable with direct, honest, respectful communication? Not always, but that's not the point. The point is to stay focused on the needs of the team, and the needs of the overall organization. To the extent that a manager is indulging their own ego, then they are making a mistake. At the risk of being overly subtle, both honest communication and dishonest communication will sometimes leave workers feeling uncomfortable, but honest communication has long-term benefits whereas dishonest communication only has long-term costs.

Can a manager use anger strategically? Maybe. Personally, I don't think it is worth the risk. If you try to use these tactics of psychological manipulation, eventually they will burn you. Your team will suffer, your organization will suffer, and your career will eventually suffer. Avoid these tactics. Direct, honest, respectful communication is always the wiser choice.

Chapter 7

Project Management

Let's start by talking about terrible project managers. I was working at a web design agency in 2008, and the project manager was not very intelligent. He was a very spiffy dresser; he constantly donned stylish shoes. If I looked down at his feet, I almost always felt envious. He traveled in Europe and acquired a collection of fantastic dress shoes from various fashion capitals. But he was unquestionably a bad manager. His disorganization would come across in conversations like this:

Him: Hey, uh, you done with Task 5 yet?

Me: No, not yet. I haven't even started on it.

Him: Oh. Shit. When are you gonna do it?

Me: I guess after tasks 2 and 3 and 4?

Him: Oh, no, listen, it's really important.

Me: Oh? Since when?

Him: Yeah, like, I just got a call from the client. They need this by tomorrow.

Me: Um, what … ? Okay well, I can do it by next week.

Him: No, listen, okay? Listen, this is really important.

Me: I can stop what I'm doing now and focus on it.

Him: Yeah, good.

Me: But I don't think it'll be done tomorrow.

Him: It's super important. You've got to get this done tomorrow.

Me: I don't think it's possible. Task 5 is really big.

Him: This is super important. They will go bankrupt if you don't get this done tomorrow.

Me: Wait, what? Uh, first of all, that can't be true, and second of all, have we been paid yet? Third of all, it isn't our responsibility to keep them in business. Fourth of all, someone could have told me that Task 5 was important? Why didn't we make it Task 1?

Him: Cool, cool, I'll tell them.

Me: Wait, what? You'll tell them what? Did you hear what I said?

And then he walks away. Two days later he comes back and we have this conversation:

Him: Hey, are you done with Task 2 yet?

Me: No, I worked 16 hours yesterday on Task 5!

Him: Don't worry about Task 5.

Me: Wait, what? I thought the client was going bankrupt without Task 5?

Him: Dude, that's not even possible. And, really, is it our responsibility to keep them in business? Anyway, Task 2 is the important thing now, can you work on that?

Me: As soon as I'm done with Task 5.

Him: Nah, c'mon, dude. Probably nobody really cares about Task 5. Can you focus on Task 2? You were supposed to be done with Task 2 by now.

Me: Yeah, if I hadn't wasted two days on Task 5, then I might be done with Task 2 by now.

Him: So, you'll get it done today?

Me: I'm very focused on Task 5, having spent many hours figuring out the nuances of the request.

Him: Yeah, man, that's some stupid marketing thing. I think it's probably been canceled. They're going to try something else.

Me: Okay, whatever. Why should I even care? I'll focus on Task 2.

Him: Okay, great.

Two days later he comes back to me and we have another conversation.

Him: Hey, man, are you done with Task 5 yet?

Me: Tell me you're kidding.

Him: C'mon man, I told you how important that was.

Me: But you also told me that Task 5 was canceled.

Him: I said I thought it was probably canceled, but you should have kept working on it till I confirmed that it was canceled. Turns out it wasn't canceled. That's your mistake.

Me: How is that my mistake? You're the one who said it was probably canceled.

Him: Yeah, "probably." You jumped the gun if you acted before that was confirmed.

Me: So you want me to work on Task 5 now?

Him: No, man, they probably went bankrupt now. They really needed it at the beginning of the week.

Me: Are they bankrupt or probably bankrupt?

Him: Oh man, what's with all the questions? Do you know how much time I waste trying to track down answers for all these questions that you ask me?

Me: I waste your time?

Him: I mean, can't you figure anything out on your own?

Me: Am I allowed to talk directly to the client?

Him: No, are you crazy? We have account specialists who talk to the clients. Engineers don't know how to talk to the clients.

Me: I could ask them simply, "Is this task your highest priority?"

Him: You don't know how to talk to clients. It's a special skill. You need to figure out what kind of pain they are suffering, and then you need to figure out how we can help them solve that pain.

Me: I could ask them, "Are you guys about to go bankrupt?" Then I could ask, "Would Task 5 help you avoid bankruptcy?"

Him: See, this is why no one enjoys talking to engineers.

Me: I'll get to work on Task 5.

Him: Thanks, man. Not sure why you had to have a meltdown over such a simple request, but thanks.

The next Monday he comes back to me again.

Him: Hey, man, uh, what are you working on?

Me: I got done with Task 5 and Task 2, so now I'm working on Task 3.

Him: Oh, man, really? That sucks.

Me: Why does that suck?

Him: Dude, Tasks 2 and 5 were definitely canceled. You were supposed to be working on Tasks 6 and 7.

Me: Why can't you keep any of this straight?

Him: Me? What are you talking about? I'm not the guy who just wasted a week working on the wrong things.

Me: If I'm not allowed to talk to the client, then I've got to depend on you to tell me what the client actually needs.

Him: I talk to the account specialist every day, and they talk to the client every day, so I've got a ton of notes about "what the client actually needs." You want to see all of my notes? I've got a ton of notes.

Me: Well, why aren't these notes being communicated to me in a timely fashion?

Him: You want to see all of my notes? Look at this! I mean, seriously, just look at this! I've got a million notes about what the client needs!

Me: Okay, look, you seem like you understand what our client needs, but you are mismanaging this project.

Him: Oh, man, what's with the insults? I always say, "If someone tries to compliment you but says the word 'but,' don't listen to anything before the 'but'." So all I just heard you say was, "You are mismanaging this project." That's mean. You're really mean, dude.

Me: Okay, how about this. You are the worst project manager in the entire history of the universe, but I like your shoes.

Him: Yeah, these are great shoes, right? I love these shoes. I got them in Europe.

The signature of a terrible project manager is that they don't actually track the project; they simply ask the people involved how things are going. By contrast, if there is one thing that a great project manager does, they develop multiple metrics by which they can track a project and confirm that real progress is actually being made. In the same way an accountant will look at multiple records to ensure a transaction was real and not fraudulent, a great project manager looks for contradictions among multiple metrics, as any contradiction will suggest that they don't yet have the full story.

What does great project management look like?

During the 22 years that I've worked in tech, the best project manager with whom I worked was at ShermansTravel.com in 2011 and 2012. Her name is Sonia Bramwell, and she oversaw the tech team — which at its peak had seven people, plus an overseas team with another six people on it. I'd like to share some of her ideas.

Here are a few attributes of a great project manager:

1. Does not allow work to proceed until all dependencies are ready

Bramwell had a rule that a worker should not start working on a task if that task needed something which had not yet been provided. For instance, a web developer might have a task such as "Change all icons in the shopping cart," but perhaps the graphic designer had not yet finished designing all of the icons. In those cases, Bramwell would ask the web developer to work on something else, while Bramwell would maintain close contact with the designer to figure out when those icons would be ready.

Even if the designer was on some different team, Bramwell would work with that other team to sort priorities in such a way that the priorities were aligned for both teams, with both understanding the urgency of any particular request. Only when the icons were ready would Bramwell let the web developer get to work on the task.

Likewise, a marketer might be asked to write text for a new product, before the top management had decided if they would position it as a premium product or a value product. In such cases, it is best to keep the marketer from wasting their time.

Every time I teach people this rule, someone responds, "You are trying to do things the old-fashioned Waterfall way, but it is much better to do things with the Agile style, where everything happens at once!" My experience with "Do everything at once" is that it leads to a lot of confusion, a lot of wasted work, and a lot of burnout. By all means, do things in parallel when you can, but if you try to take fundamentally sequential tasks and treat them as tasks that can be done in parallel, the end result tends to be frustration.

Most of the time, no one should be asked to work on a task when that task depends on work that has not yet been done.

2. Overcomes the inertia of the company's bureaucracy

In a sense, this simply re-states the previous point in a different way — when the company fails to deliver the resources that a worker needs, the project manager finds those resources.

In a poorly run company, workers struggle to get the credentials, services, permissions or access that they need to do their job. In such a company, you'll hear computer programmers complaining, "They told us we were now going to be responsible for fixing problems in production, but so far no one has given us access to the production environment." Or you will hear someone on the marketing team complain, "I'm supposed to improve our sales conversion process, but so far no one has given me access to our analytics platform, so I have no way to make changes, or even begin doing an analysis of the problem."

Entire weeks are wasted this way. Productivity is low. Projects are always behind schedule.

Sometimes companies end up like this because they are trying to be flat, so they don't have many managers, and the managers are therefore stretched thin. Managerial responsibilities are then dumped onto the workers, but often the workers are not empowered to actually fulfill those responsibilities.

I once started at a company and one of my top tasks was to improve the performance of the database. Yet it took the leadership six weeks to get me a username and password for the database. While that is an extreme case, it also reveals how pervasive the problem can be. I had very little to do for my first six weeks.

A well-run company hires great project managers, and then those project managers gather up all of the resources and permissions that the workers need to do their job, so the workers do not waste hours or days (or even weeks) trying to get what they need to do the work.

3. Fearlessly defends the team from both management and clients

This rule could also be phrased as, "Fearlessly defends the development process from arbitrary changes."

When ShermansTravel.com was at its peak, circa 2008, it had 80 employees but it had outsourced all software development work. The management found outsourcing to be expensive and slow, so they decided to bring some of the software development work in-house. They hired one software developer, then two, then three. There was no team leader and no structure. When the CEO wanted some change made to the website or the newsletter, they would walk over to one of the software developers and ask them to drop whatever they were doing and instead focus on the task the CEO now felt was important (à la the dialogue I shared at the beginning of this chapter). Likewise, if the head of marketing needed a change made urgently, they would simply walk over to an engineer and ask them to drop everything else and focus on making the one change that the head of marketing wanted. Utter chaos reigned and the software became an unholy mess that no software developer could truly understand. There was no effort at a cohesive architecture, nor was anyone in charge of making long-term technical decisions.

When Bramwell was hired, she was young and uncertain — but after a few years she had become confident, and she was now a warrior who was ready to fight anyone who messed with her team. A good process was developed for deciding which tasks were important and which were less important. Bramwell defended the process, which is to say, she defended the manner in which decisions were made. She vehemently resisted sudden, arbitrary changes to the plan. The team then worked in two-week sprints, and if some manager wanted to change the tasks halfway through a sprint, Bramwell would put the request through a rigorous vetting process. Only real emergencies were allowed to change the tasks that the software developers were working on.

There are moments when it is useful to have the engineers (or any kind of staff with specific skills) talk to upper management and outside clients. But those discussions need to go through a particular process; they can not be allowed to happen randomly.

Hopefully everyone already knows this, but I'll say it again just in case someone inexperienced has not heard this before: allowing the CEO to make any request of any person at any time is not healthy for an organization. It will lead to chaos and weaken the organization. A smart CEO knows this. A smart CEO knows that any large organization needs development processes, and the processes need to be held as sacred, and exceptions to a process need to be very rare. The people who work for an organization need to fight for the long-term needs of the organization, not for the CEO, who might only be around for five or six years. Occasionally some particular CEO gets angry at me when I'm too vocal about this, but everyone aside from the CEO typically understands the wisdom of what I'm saying.

4. Not afraid of the technical side

A project manager is not a computer programmer, not a marketer, and not a designer, but the best project managers are not afraid of the technical side of the work. They are willing to learn the basics of whatever skills are central to the team they're overseeing, if only to be more insightful about the deeper aspects of the craft.

This applies to teams that have nothing to do with software development. A project manager at a construction firm will also be good with spreadsheets and might even learn how to write Excel macros, because they will need spreadsheets to keep track of finances and other resources.

At ShermansTravel.com, we used SQL to talk to the databases. Bramwell never got to the point where she could write SQL from scratch, but she did get to the point where she could modify it when she needed to. This was no more complicated than, say, working with Excel functions, and again, she was not afraid of the technical side of things.

Assume we needed to send out a newsletter, but only to those users who were at least 18 years old. Bramwell was willing to learn this much SQL:

```
SELECT first_name, last_name, date_of_birth, email
FROM users
WHERE date_of_birth < '2001-07-04' ORDER BY
date_of_birth
```

Here, Bramwell could see the year, and as the years went by, she could adjust the year and the date to be sure she was always seeing the list of users who were at least 18 years old as of that current day. Before we'd send out a newsletter, she might run such a query and inspect the list of users that were generated. And when someone reported that there was an error, she would run the query and try to diagnose the problem herself, then figure out who she should assign the problem to, or assess whether the problem was even real.

Every time an engineer wrote some SQL for her, Bramwell would save it to a wiki and write a note about how it worked. Over time, she got better and better at using SQL. She was never an engineer, but she was never afraid to pick up what she could about the technical side of the work.

Also, this is a somewhat subtle point but I'll mention it here: At most companies people will focus their energy on what gets them promoted. If the project manager has any influence on whether the engineer gets promoted, then it especially helps the morale of the team if the project manager has a nuanced appreciation of the technical aspects of the work. In particular, if a given task takes much longer than expected, the engineer will want to be working for a project manager who can understand the task well enough that they understand when the delay was not the fault of the engineer.

5. Analyzes team members and knows when they are lying or boasting

Here I'll restrict my remarks to software development teams. Most computer programmers tend to be a bit macho about their abilities. Ask a computer programmer, "How long will it take you to get done with Task 3?" and if a reasonable answer is "five hours," then the computer programmer says "three hours." Oddly competitive, they like to strut around pretending they are faster than anyone else.

At the same time, there are some computer programmers who are afraid of getting blamed for a task that goes over time and over budget, so they offer bloated estimates. Ask them how long it will take them to do Task 3 and they will say "ten hours."

When I was at ShermansTravel.com, Bramwell did a remarkable job of parsing each computer programmer and figuring out if they were the type of person who would boast or lie. She then adjusted their estimates accordingly. She knew that with some programmers, if they said "three hours," then she should mark the task as a five-hour task, whereas with other programmers, if they said a task would take ten hours, then she should mark the task as a five-hour task.

This is the very subtle human element of project management. I don't think it can be taught in school, but it can be learned from years of experience interacting with various people on various projects. One way to accelerate your own learning process is to make predictions, before any work is done, about each computer programmer and each task — then carefully measure how wrong you were, and update your understanding of people accordingly. Be systematic about this.

6. Finds multiple ways to keep track of progress

As I demonstrated in the dialogue at the beginning of the chapter, the worst project managers tend to keep track of a project simply by going up to members of the team and asking, "Hey, you done yet?"

It's good to check directly with team members, but it's also important to have other ways of checking on progress. The following are a few such techniques.

- If Team Member A needs to work with other people on the team, ask those other people if they've collaborated with Team Member A yet.
- If Team Member A is doing research on a project, assume that research is being gathered somewhere online, and then check that source — maybe it's a wiki, or Google Docs, or Dropbox, or Basecamp, or a chatroom. Has research been done? Ask that they share their notes in a public place, or update you daily via email.
- If Team Member A is writing software, then their software will typically go into some kind of version control system — look at that version control system and see if there have been updates from Team Member A. In some companies, all resources, including design ar-

tifacts and spreadsheets, are saved to a central version control system, so it's possible to keep track of all of these things.

- If Team Member A is brainstorming creative ideas, again, encourage them to keep those online so you can check on them. (But don't be critical of early ideas.)
- If Team Member A helps with sales, you probably have a CRM, and you probably ask Team Member A to record things in the CRM, and they probably hate the CRM, because all salespeople hate whatever CRM they're asked to use. At some point they have to enter data into the CRM, but as a temporary and partial solution, encourage them to use the Voice To Text feature on their phone to send you email.
- If Team Member A is building something like software, try to use the software as soon as possible.

In other words, a good project manager works towards having a 360° vision on what their team members are doing. A project manager who simply asks people, "Are you done yet?" is a failure.

Many companies don't have a role explicitly labeled "project management." Instead, the role is subsumed into other roles, such as, for marketing, the Vice President of Marketing or Assistant Vice President of Marketing. That's fine, so long as someone knows they have this responsibility and does it well.

7. Assertively confronts underperforming team members

Great project managers are polite but direct. If someone repeatedly misses targets, a great project manager will ask them why. No doubt the person will have many excuses. It is important to drill down past all of the excuses. None of the excuses matter; all that matters is the question, to be put to the failing team member, "What needs to change so that you live up to expectations?" A great project manager knows how to remain polite, while also pushing hard to get that question answered.

8. Fearlessly fires those team members who fail to improve

This comment is mostly for the U.S., where managers are granted considerable freedom to fire people. Obviously one doesn't want to build a company where people are fired for arbitrary reasons, as that would be unethical and would also damage morale which can cause the best people to quit. But when you've worked with someone to improve their performance and they have not improved, a good project manager will try to protect the rest of the team by getting rid of those who have disappointed the team repeatedly.

9. Speaks well when in front of an audience

A project manager will constantly be defending their team to upper management, and then, later on, they will be defending the wishes of upper management to their team. It is essential that a project manager can feel comfortable when in front of small groups. It is rare that a project manager needs to talk to a packed stadium with 1,000 people in it, but talking to groups of 10 to 30 people is something that project managers will do often. They need to be able to speak clearly, speak loudly, speak candidly, never get flustered by tough questions, and always be polite but firm, even when someone is being aggressive towards them. Fortunately, this is something they can definitely learn to do, if they don't already know how.

What about Scrum, Agile, Kanban, PMP and CAPM?

At this point many of you will be wondering, where is the conversation about all of the formal methodologies? Some of you will think it's strange that I've written a whole chapter about project management without mentioning Scrum, Agile, Kanban, PMP and CAPM. I have three responses:

1. There are many books that teach each of these methodologies, so if you want to study a specific methodology, you should pick up one of those specialized books.

2. Many of those methodologies seem optimized for large corporations, whereas I'm offering advice for small- and medium-sized businesses.

3. The benefits of the formal methodologies are unclear.

Let's dig into this last part.

I have not personally noticed that credentials (such as Scrum Master or PMP) are necessarily associated with real skill as a project manager. Rather, the key things that make a great project manager tend to be more qualitative:

- Does this person have the moral convictions necessary to take a tough stand against upper management, for the benefit of the overall company?
- Does this person have the confidence necessary to fire a poor performer for the benefit of the overall team?
- Does this person have the perceptiveness to correctly read team members and know when they are lying or boasting?

Certain people gain these attributes as they gain experience, but these attributes tend to be things that are not emphasized in formal credentialed courses. Strong moral convictions tend to be picked up in childhood and are only learned slowly in adulthood. In formal credentialed courses the focus on various rote processes tends to shift the focus away from the things that are really important. Consider the point made by Greg Jorgensen:

> Whether a methodology works or not depends on the criteria: team productivity, happiness, retention, conformity, predictability, accountability, communication, lines per day, man-months, code quality, artifacts produced, etc. Every methodology works if you measure the right thing. But in terms of the only measurement that really matters — satisfying requirements on time and within budget — I haven't seen any methodology deliver consistent results.

https://typicalprogrammer.com/
why-dont-software-development-methodologies-work

This is my experience as well. The formal programs that describe themselves as "Agile" do not deliver consistent results. Occasionally they seem to work very well, but the success of those projects might be due to other factors. And occasionally these formal methodologies do not work at all.

So how is a company to achieve excellent project management, if formal credentials and formal programs are not a good guide to success? This goes back to hiring and training. When you have the time, you can hire a novice and let them grow into the role. Bramwell was hired as a novice and later developed an excellent talent. Other times you'll want to hire someone who is already fully formed as a project manager. There, getting recommendations from those who have worked with them is the most important thing. It might take some effort to talk to a range of people who have worked with the person over the years. Again, you'll be looking for stories that convince you that this is a person who has the appropriate toughness and moral certainty, mentioned previously.

It takes a lot of work to hire a great project manager, but it is worth it.

Chapter 8

The cost of attrition: don't lose your best people

Great news! You just raised a round of investment! You are flush with cash! Now you can hit those ambitious goals that you excitedly promised to your investors. In six months, you can go back and tell them that you totally crushed the numbers — not only did you *make* your milestones, you blew past them. The investors will be so pleased! Now we just need to tell your head of marketing to ramp up the customer acquisition! Luckily she has a genius for this kind of thing. Oh, wait, here she is now, walking over to you, about to say ...

... oh damn. She just quit? That was unexpected.

One-on-one meetings are useful for many things, one of which is that you aren't likely to be ambushed by a surprise resignation. There are many personal issues that might cause someone to quit, and these will never, ever be mentioned in a group meeting. Burnout? A divorce? A spouse with a job in a different city? A child failing in school? A parent who is dying? Interest in other kinds of work? No one shouts that stuff in a group meeting, but they might tell you when you are one-on-one.

Or consider what Benji Webber wrote:

You have a team. Someone leaves. We hire a replacement. We get lucky and manage to find someone more skilled. Looks like we're better off?

Really when someone leaves we lose all the relationships they had with the rest of the team as well. The team is diminished more like 40% than the apparent 20%. It takes longer to rebuild the team than is apparent. Relationships take time.

https://benjiweber.co.uk/blog/2022/01/12/cost-of-attrition/

One-on-one meetings are a fantastic way to lower your rate of attrition. When you have these kinds of conversations, you can form the kinds of relationships which make it less likely that your best people will leave — and you can almost completely eliminate the situation where they leave without warning.

As Webber says, relationships take time. And work is fundamentally about human relationships.

Chapter 9

How to hire

Hiring is a huge topic and here we can only scratch the surface with a few general observations. Every profession will have concerns that are unique, and specialized resources should be consulted when hiring for those professions. Here we focus on hiring for small teams at small- and medium-sized startups.

There is currently a craving in the business world to come up with the perfect formula for hiring. "Follow these seven rules and everyone you hire will turn out great." Go on Twitter or Medium or Substack, and you'll see advice that makes it sound easy: "To eliminate risk, to eliminate variance, to eliminate confusion, just do these simple things."

However, this craving for a formula is misguided. Hiring is an art; not a science. Whereas science promises repeatable results, hiring the perfect person every time is only possible when you have the equivalent of a master craftsperson who is doing the hiring. That is, someone who listens carefully to everything they're being told while also noticing everything that is left untold. Someone who can find the nugget of truth hidden in silence.

Practice makes perfect, at golf, at pottery and also at hiring. You will get better at hiring the more you do it. Still, as with golf or art, there are some rough rules of thumb to keep in mind as you practice. These rules are not a scientific formula that always works, but if you practice with them in mind, you'll find they are useful, and over time you'll adapt them to your own circumstances. Keep track of what you were thinking when you made each hire; keep track of how the person succeeds or disappoints you. Over time, you'll get better and better at picking winners with every hire.

The efficacy of social proof

When hiring, I rely heavily on recommendations from people I know, or at least know of. To use some Silicon Valley jargon, I rely on "social proof." If a good engineer with whom I've worked recommends some other engineer or project manager or product manager, that counts for a lot with me.

I recently tweeted this idea on Twitter and James Youngman responded, "It seems to me that this kind of approach is what perpetuates the domination of the industry by an in-group (who know each other, directly or indirectly) at the expense of outsiders, to the detriment of both diversity and fairness."

That's a valid concern. We all have a professional and ethical obligation to be sure that we hire a diverse workforce; that is, the workforce must be open to anyone who has real talent. In my experience, there is no contradiction between that obligation and a requirement that a candidate be recommended by someone we trust. Assuming you have friends and colleagues who understand their professional and ethical obligations the same way you do, they should be able to give recommendations on people they know or put you in touch with friends of theirs who can offer such recommendations. Within your extended social penumbra of friends, friends of friends, and friends of friends of friends, you should be able to find someone who can vouch for most of the candidates that you need to hire. You just need to put in the effort, chasing down those recommendations through extended chains of acquaintances.

This approach very much works when you are hiring novices who are straight out of school. It helps to stay in touch with friends and colleagues who are teaching or mentoring at schools or the software developer bootcamps. Back in 2018, when I needed some junior-level frontend software developers, I hired several women from the Grace Hopper program for women that is run by Fullstack Academy. In that case I spoke with some experienced friends of mine who had either taught at the school or volunteered as mentors. As such, they could point me to those who were the best of the graduating class and I ended up with an unusually excellent team of novices.

"But this will never scale!"

Again on Twitter, several people suggested that such a method can work at a small startup with maybe a hundred people, but not at a large company. In response, I pointed out that if I have a successful career of 40 years, I will, at most, interview maybe 3,000 people, and hire perhaps 500 or 600 people. That is, in my full work life, the numbers I deal with will be personal and small-scale. It does not matter if I am at a small startup or the CEO of Microsoft, I will still only directly hire a few hundred people during my whole career.

Another Twitter user responded, "Hiring friends of friends only works for you, personally. We need a system that works in the general case."

I disagree. There is no "general case" when it comes to hiring. You are always a specific person, living in a specific country during a specific year, and you are hiring another specific person for a specific job. You are not hiring an abstract entity. Even factory workers on an assembly line are not fungible: that is why some of them get promoted and some don't, while others get fired. They are each different. You are hiring someone with specific life experiences, who comes to you from a specific context and who delivers to you some unique mix of skills that only they have. If you blind yourself to this truth, you will do fantastic amounts of damage to your organization.

I acknowledge, there is currently a debate over how big companies should hire. Should hiring be a centralized process run by the Human Resources team, or should each team be allowed to follow its own rules when hiring? This question goes to a larger issue: how much should the company be made legible to those at the top? We know that leaders must delegate some authority and we also know that the demand to make the organization legible only to the top can add unnecessary layers of bureaucracy and paperwork. However, the leadership does have a responsibility to understand the risks that the organization is facing as a whole. What is the ideal balance of these factors? There is no easy answer. In every case, it is an empirical question, to be discovered experimentally.

This book is aimed mostly at entrepreneurs of small to medium sized companies. For you, the truth is simple: you are hiring a specific individual, not an abstract entity. As such, try to find references who know the job candidate, who can speak to their strengths and weaknesses. In your entire life, you will only directly hire a limited number of people, so devote yourself fully to each hiring decision.

Be careful about the money you invest into recruiters

Nowadays, even at small startups, there is a tendency to rely on recruiters to bring in job candidates. Every recruiter claims they know of a secret, unique source of talent, and yet every recruiter is actually just scouring LinkedIn and Indeed, and then randomly contacting people and asking them if they are looking for work. Seriously, I get five to ten spam emails each week, from recruiters who found me on LinkedIn and are wondering if I'd like a new job.

Even in friendly settings, talking with recruiters at the bar or at a party of mutual acquaintances, I've yet to meet a recruiter who goes beyond the major jobs boards. What surprises me is that they do not do what I do, which is keep in close contact with some schools and dev bootcamps. Why not? Apparently it just isn't worth it to them: they don't get extra money for finding the ideal candidate, they don't lose money if they waste a company's time with a dozen candidates who are a poor fit.

Recruiters are typically paid 20% of the first year's salary of a hired recruit. If you hire a software engineer for $200,000, you'll pay the recruiter $40,000. But consider how many better candidates you might get if you offered a salary of $240,000 instead? My sense is that most startup leaders have not thought carefully about how much they lose when they pay so much to recruiters, money that could go to one's own staff instead.

At every startup that I've worked for, the leadership complains that recruiters are bringing them junk candidates. For the recruiters, hiring is simply a numbers game – if they bring enough candidates to enough companies, then someone, some-where, will eventually hire the candidate. Quality? There is little incentive to find above average workers for you. The transactional nature of recruitment hiring tends to hurt everyone in the system. I'm aware of efforts to find a new model, but so far such efforts are embryonic.

As a leader, part of your job is hiring. If you are not hiring now, then you will be hiring in the future. Once you fully internalize that reality, you'll also realize that you need to build connections to potential sources of recruits. Constantly. This might entail collecting business cards at professional conferences, or making contacts at the various events or Meetups you go to, or keeping contacts at universities and dev bootcamps. Another source of future talent is startup incubators – because most start-ups fail, many of the people working at a startup incubator will be in need of a new job about a year from now. If you've read my book, *How To Destroy A Tech Startup In Three Easy Steps*, you'll remember exactly that happened at the NYU Tandon startup incubator on Varick Street. After I left the start-up I was working for, I kept in touch with the people there and later I did indeed hire one of them.

Be careful about the time you invest into the big job boards

Some companies avoid recruiters, in which case they use the major job boards directly. They then get inundated by the flood of job applicants who spam every possible job opening. This is even more inefficient than relying on recruiters, who, despite all of their failings, do screen out some of the worst candidates. I am left again wondering why leaders at small to medium sized businesses don't reach out to more obvious sources of talent, such as schools and startup incubators.

Using a big jobs board seems very convenient, at least at first. You type up your job description, and post it, and voila, literally millions of job applicants can now see your job posting! Amazing! It's so easy to get started! Until the inevitable flood of applicants inundates your inbox.

Yet somehow, the whole industry goes on in this habit, and seems committed to it. It is not an exaggeration to say I've had several conversations almost exactly like this:

Them: I'm trying to fill a position and I put up a job posting at LinkedIn and Indeed and StackOverflow.

Me: Did you get any candidates that you like?

Them: Well, actually, I've gotten several thousand. The problem is trying to narrow down the pile. I can't look through all of them. I've decided to post the job a second time, but this time I created a quiz that people have to take.

Me: What is the quiz about?

Them: It's 100 questions about the technologies we use, plus some algorithm questions that should help cut down the number of applicants who get through.

Me: You created the questions yourself?

Them: No, I copied and pasted them from various on-line sources. Most of them are about standard stuff.. I put in a few obscure trick questions to help filter out the weak candidates.

Me: Are you sure that is what you need, people who happen to know some fairly obscure stuff?

Them: Well, not really. Our work here is fairly standard, but I need some way to filter the applicants — because, as I said, the first time I posted the job we got way too many responses.

Me: How many people do you need to hire?

Them: I need three developers for the frontend, and two more for the backend.

Me: That seems like a manageable number. Have you tried to find some good candidates from friends or acquaintances?

Them: Oh, I don't have time for that. We need to move quickly with these hires.

Me: Is talking with friends any slower than making up quiz-zes for Indeed?

Them: Well, I'm not sure how I would even start.

Me: Just call a friend and ask them if they know anyone looking for a job?

Them: You mean, like, I pick up a phone and then I'm like, "Hi, Jill, I need three developers for the frontend, and two more for the backend, do you know anyone?"

Me: Exactly.

Them: But what if she doesn't know anyone?

Me: Call someone else? You do have more than one friend, right?

Them: So, wait, just go through my contacts randomly calling people?

Me: No, not randomly. If you have a friend who is an NBA superstar, that's very cool, but their opinion about frontenders shouldn't carry too much weight. Focus on people in your industry, starting with people you've worked with.

Them: And just call them?

Me: Or text them. Or send them an email. Or post the notice on Facebook and Twitter. The goal is to get someone recommended by someone whose reputation you know. Anyone they recommend should be given priority over some random resume that comes in through Indeed.

Them: Hmm, I worry it would feel like I'm asking for a favor.

Me: That's exactly what you are doing, you are asking for a favor. And then later on, when they need something, maybe you can do them a favor. That's how favors work.

Them: I don't know, man. That sounds like it would take a lot of time.

Me: Compared to what? Reading through a thousand resumes from Indeed?

Them: This whole hiring thing really sucks, you know? I mean, no matter what, it takes a lot of effort and I've got other work to do. Instead I have to waste time doing this.

Me: Hiring is important work, right? This is important for the future of your team.

Them: Sure, I guess that's true, but I've also got a lot of software that I'm supposed to write.

Me: As your team grows, you'll need to spend less time writing code and more time focused on management tasks, such as hiring people, right?

Them: Yeah, but that's a lot easier said than done. You should see some of the resumes that I got – full of typos, obvious exaggerations, stuff that makes no sense. The applicants we're getting from these online sites, most of them are really awful.

Me: It sounds like Indeed isn't really giving you what you want.

Them: That's true, Indeed sucks.

Me: So, maybe you'll reach out to your acquaintances and

ask them for recommendations?

Them: Oh, gosh, no. Like I said, that would take too much time.

For many categories of job applicants, job sites like Monster or LinkedIn or Indeed or StackOverflow offer such an abundance of material that you are tricked into thinking, "Surely we can feed endlessly from this source." Yet they waste so much of your time that they are effectively a kind of productivity poison. Please consider that the convenience they offer is actually a kind of anti-convenience once you consider how much spam will waste your time.

If you devote just a few days per year to maintaining ties with universities and other schools, you'll have direct access to a far more qualified pool of talent, from the 19 year old looking for a summer internship to the 29 year old finishing their Masters degree to the 39 year old adjunct professor who you can hire for much more than the university pays them.

Homework assignments and personality quizzes won't give you excellence

This year I was once again hiring junior-level developers, and the same dynamic was at work, but I got a surprising reaction from the person I spoke to. I'll call her Zareen, who had just come through the Fullstack Academy Grace Hopper program.

Zareen had been interviewing at a few different places, but I assumed she was still open to hearing about the specific job that I was hiring for, so we arranged a phone call. We chatted for 15 minutes; this phone call was simply so I could see if she was interested in the kind of job we were offering and that the salary was roughly in line with what she was hoping for. Then I suggested she come to the office and interview with the whole team.

"Wow, I didn't expect things to move this fast!" she exclaimed.

Let's think about that for a minute. She wants a job, I might want to hire her, I ask her to come by the office for an interview, and she's stunned. It says a lot about how broken our hiring processes have become if what used to be the absolutely standard process now provokes the response, "Wow, I didn't expect things to move this fast!"

Apparently other companies were giving her homework assignments and personality quizzes and phone interviews. "Please go to this website and take this test, as we are trying to figure out what your skills are."

At two other companies, she had already done 20-minute phone interviews, but never with anyone on the tech team. Instead she got a call from someone in the HR department, who read a checklist of words and clearly didn't understand any of them. Nevertheless, they were all requirements: "Have you ever heard of HTML? Do you know how to use that? What about CSS? Do you have that? How many years of skill do you have with CSS? And Java? I mean, Javascript? Are those different? Yes? Okay, I think we want Javascript. Do you have that? Yes? How many years?"

What an empty ritual, reading words that are not understood.

Stupid, angry, incompetent CEOs are your friends, if they lead some other company

The tech world is full of badly run companies that receive massive rounds of investment from VC firms. Such companies have the ability to hire great talent, which is often wasted as many of these businesses eventually go bankrupt. Keep tabs on struggling firms that have great talent.

(Recently I served as the Fractional CTO for Pair Eyewear, and during that time Freshly was going through a rough spot. We hired one person from Freshly, and they were terrific. They told us that many other people at Freshly wanted to jump ship. So we ended up eventually hiring nine people from Freshly, and they were all terrific.)

I've had actual conversations like this with two friends over lunch:

Me: Hi, Sue, Kwan, good to see you. Hey, listen, I'm trying to hire for my tech team. Do you know anyone who might want a job?

Sue: Sorry, I don't know anyone.

Kwan: No. I don't know anyone, either.

Me: You can't recommend anyone at all? Anyone you think is good, or a novice who has ambition? I'm hiring both experienced and junior-level jobs. Backend, frontend, devops, project managers, I need it all.

Kwan: Sorry, man, I can't think of anyone. You should have talked to me three months ago when SugarLoveMusic flamed out. What a freaking disaster. I knew folks then.

Me: What happened at SugarLoveMusic?

Sue: Everything. Everything happened at SugarLoveMusic.

Kwan: Literally everything happened at SugarLoveMusic.

Me: Wow. I remember that you worked there, Kwan, but I didn't know you worked there, too, Sue.

Sue: For a while. Then I quit. I heard about the final days from Kwan and our friend Beatrice. She was so burned out she took a 90-day vacation. A great devops person, but they had her working 100 hours a week. Everything was chaotic.

Kwan: The CEO was a loser. Such a loser.

Sue: Yes, the CEO was unprofessional, in both his leadership and his handling of money.

Kwan: Such a loser.

Sue: Yes. We kept telling him that we needed clear guidelines about the priorities for the tech team, but he was inconsistent. He said one thing one week and then something very different the next week. He couldn't make up his mind.

Kwan: Such a loser.

Sue: The series A investors promised to put in more money if our CEO could hit certain milestones in terms of monthly subscribers. We could have done it if we'd had better cooperation between the tech team and the marketing team. They needed to run a lot of A/B tests and they needed our help with that. But communication broke down.

Me: Why did communication break down?

Sue: Our CEO kept yelling at Yin Ji, who was our project manager. She was a genius, but she couldn't take all the abuse, and in the end she quit because she just couldn't stand him anymore.

Me: Wow, that's awful. Sounds like the CEO sabotaged the whole startup?

Kwan: Such a loser.

Sue: Yes, one by one, he drove everyone to quit. I think I felt the worst for poor Egan. It was his first job ever. He showed a lot of promise as a frontender, but he was just learning and the stress really got him. He was one of the last to quit. No, wait, he might still be there.

Me: So SugarLoveMusic is still in business? I thought you said it flamed out?

Sue: Well, it ran low on money, and they had to let a lot of people go. The CEO had assumed that investors were going to give him more money, so he was kind of reckless with ... well, basically all pecuniary matters.

Me: What an idiot!

Kwan: Loser.

Me: Right, I meant loser.

Sue: I think for the investors, the final straw was when Stratton quit. He was our main backend guy, he knew a lot about file compression. When potential investors heard that Stratton had quit, it was a huge red flag.

Me: It must have been hard for Stratton, too, right? I know how rough it can be to quit suddenly like that, with nothing set up for the future.

Sue: Yeah, and I don't think he had a lot of savings. He had to take some stupid job at a dating app, doing minor tweaks to their database queries, but I don't think he loves it.

Me: No love at the love app?

Sue: He'd swipe left if he could, but he needs the job.

Me: I'm glad you two got away from that place.

Sue: Oh, yes, I'm much happier now. That CEO had really mismanaged the place.

Kwan: Such a —

Me: Loser, yes.

Kwan: I was going to say "thumb biter."

Me: Thumb biter?

Kwan: It's British.

Me: Oh … are you British?

Kwan: My mother is British.

Me: Right. Well, he sounds like a real thumb biter.

Sue: He was that as well.

Me: So, listen, you two have been a huge help. I'm grateful for all of the recommendations.

Sue: But we didn't recommend anyone.

Me: You said Beatrice is great at devops, Yin Ji is a genius project manager, Egan is a solid junior level frontender, and Stratton is a great backender. That's the team I want to hire.

Sue: Oh, but some of them already have jobs.

Me: Doesn't matter. I might be able to offer them more money, or I can offer them more interesting types of work, or I can offer them flexible hours, or I can offer a work-from-home option, or I can offer to let them work with a technology they'd like to learn — or if they want to go into management, I can offer to mentor them towards the management track. I'll be creative. I'm confident I can offer them something better than whatever they have now.

Sue: That's probably true. At the very least, you won't scream and yell like our previous CEO.

Kwan: Such a loser.

Me: Thumb biter.

Kwan: Total thumb biter. Except he had really great taste in shoes. I envied his shoes. He bought them in Europe.

Me: Wait …

The point is, if you listen carefully, almost any conversation with friends in the industry will reveal possible sources of discontent in someone's career. Keep track of these people, and keep track of their discontent. The next time you are ready to hire, you'll already have people in mind, people you've already largely decided to hire, based on what you heard from mutual friends and acquaintances.

There is a sense in which terrible CEOs are a gift. So long as they run someone else's company, and not yours, they can provide you with a steady stream of talent, as the best people will be constantly quitting from those firms.

If someone is recommending you, you weren't miserable to work with

Amanda Nock, a tech leader and devops expert who posts

frequently to Twitter, offered this in response to something I tweeted: "Another angle to professional recommendations is the social aspect, that is, if someone is recommending you, you weren't miserable to work with. When I hire, I generally don't expect people to know every tool and library and language we use, but I do care that they have the tech fundamentals, they're not miserable to work with, and they're willing to learn."

Exactly. If I can talk to someone who has worked with or mentored a candidate, I can ask about the subtle factors, beyond mere skill, that determine whether they will work out. Zareen was recommended to me by one of her mentors, who was also a friend of mine. I got to ask my friend what they thought of Zareen's ability to learn quickly, to work with others, and to communicate clearly. An acquaintance's recommendation saves many hours of work you otherwise need to invest to learn about a person.

At another company Zareen got to speak to the head of the frontend Web team, who was excited to share his special homework assignment with her: "Okay, very good, I want you to go to my page on Github, I'm sending you the link right now, I want you to download that, follow the installation procedures that I've outlined in the README, then I want you to study this for a while and then tell me why it's broken. I've embedded five bugs in the software, it's your job to find them and fix them all. You must be able to do this by tomorrow, okay, we need to see that you are eager to get this done. This should be easy for you. We are looking for people who can handle this easily."

Ah, yes, the ambush homework assignment that takes over your evening, no matter what else you had planned. If you really want to impress this one company, you will cancel your schedule and instead focus on this homework assignment – unpaid. Of course, the company with this style of hiring doesn't necessarily get the best people, but rather, they get people whose social calendar tends to be empty. Furthermore, the company is sending a loud signal: "We believe we have the right to impose on your schedule whenever we wish." The company will only get those candidates who are desperate enough to accept such impositions.

How objective is your objective test?

In the tech industry, I've seen good people, full of good intentions, invest serious time in developing what they felt was an unbiased, fact-based system of hiring, yet they were blind to the extent that their own preferences were being treated as facts. They seem to have a fear that nuance, subtlety, reasonableness and proportionality are all subjective and introduce bias into the process, even though it is impossible to hire well without considering nuances that are extremely subtle.

In 2010, I was looking for a job and I interviewed at a place that was developing in-browser games. Their backend code was entirely written in PHP, and their lead programmer, who I'll call Boris, was also one of the founders. A few people chatted with me, and then I had an interview with Boris himself. He said they were making an effort to clean up some of their code base, and then he brought some of the code up on a big screen and asked me what improvements I would make.

The code was shockingly bad, with multiple 'for' loops in each function. A simplified version looked like this:

```
$results = array();
$users = getUsers();

for ($i=0; $i < count($users); $i++) {
    $results[] = is_inactive_user($users[$i]);
}

$users = null;
$i = null;
```

```
for ($j=0; $j < count($results); $j++) {
    archive_inactive_user($results[$j]);
}
```

I asked, "Why are $users and $i set to null after the first 'for' loop?"

He answered, "Oh, I got bitten many times by variables that leaked from one part of the function to another part of the function, so I got in the habit of explicitly canceling all variables when I'm done using them."

Everything about this was terrible. I told him he urgently needed to get each 'for' loop into its own function. He made some very stupid remark in reply, about too many function calls hurting performance. If I'd allowed myself to speak freely I might have said something like, Uh, okay, if performance is a concern then why are you using a slow language like PHP? Why not switch to a faster language?

He showed me another bit of code that looked like the above, but without the variables being canceled after the loops. How would I clean this up, he asked.

"I'd move every 'for' loop to its own function," I said.

But that wasn't what he wanted to hear. He wanted me to say, "You should cancel each variable after each loop."

Needless to say, I didn't get the job, nor did I want the job. He was looking to hire software developers who would be willing to follow his idiosyncratic and unprofessional style. I wasn't interested.

I tell this story when I'm being critical of certain kinds of coding tests, and hiring managers respond, "Well, that is an extreme and ridiculous example." It is indeed extreme and ridiculous, therefore, it's easy to see the problem. Yet, even when tests are less idiosyncratic than that one, they will still reflect the values, skills, and aesthetics of the person doing the hiring. How could they not? Anyone who hires someone for their team will want someone who is at least somewhat consonant with the style and goals of the team. Wanting that consonance is reasonable, up to a point. Certainly, when I hire, I'm looking for someone who either shares my aesthetics or is willing to learn my aesthetics. That is, I explicitly recognize that there are subjective factors that shape hiring decisions.

Whenever I say this, I get pushback from people who say some variation of, "This is why tech remains exclusive, with a dominant in-group that never changes, because the people with the power to hire only hire those who are just like them."

I, however, would say the opposite is true. The only way to make the profession of software development (or the profession of marketing or operations or sales or law or any other profession) more diverse is to explicitly recognize that all hiring contains a subjective element, and that one of the goals of hiring must be the creation of a diverse workforce, open to anyone with real talent. Only after you've explicitly recognized that there are subjective factors that shape hiring can you explicitly move to build a diverse workforce. By contrast, the pretense of objective tests has too often served as a smokescreen behind which lurk forces that conserve the status quo.

If the moral urgency of this issue leaves you unmoved, consider the practical element: everything you need to know about a candidate you can learn from recommendations and by talking to the candidate. If you ask them direct questions, and you ask follow up questions until you are sure you know everything that you need to know, then you will discover what you need without wasting time on tests. This is faster for you, and it is faster for the candidate, and therefore this is both more fair and more efficient for everyone.

This is not to say that I never use tests. I use tests all the time. Not because they are objective, but for the opposite reason: they often reveal some of the subjective factors that are essential for making good hiring decisions. If I am interviewing a junior level software developer, and I give them a challenge that only a senior level software developer could handle, I'm not actually looking to see if this developer can do the work. I know they can't. I am looking to see if they panic, or if they remain calm and ask me all of the questions that they should be asking me.

What are the key questions you should ask a job candidate?

For every profession or skillset, there are typically a few questions that reveal important truths about a person's seriousness. In his book *The Seven Habits of Highly Effective People*, Steven Covey suggested that when hiring a salesperson, ask them what their favorite self-help books are — because if they don't read self-help books, they're probably not building a career in sales.

Another example was offered when I posted on Twitter about how to hire good people, and Amanda Nock responded with, "When I hire remotely, I ask about their online friends." Nock doesn't need the details of anyone's online friendships, but she needs to know that the person can communicate easily and naturally online, otherwise working with them remotely is going to be difficult.

Nock says, "When I hire remotely, I make a point to ask about what people's online lives are like. No details. If someone, for instance, has good relationships on Twitter or they're active in a Discord server, that tells me they're good at asynchronous remote communication. I don't care if the Discord server they're active in is a furry community or whatever, the details don't matter — the skill for forming relationships and communicating in a personable way over asynchronous text is there."

Another bit of advice comes from Lindsey Allard, co-founder and co-leader of the very successful PlaybookUX: "I make a list of five critical things that the person must have, and then I don't compromise at all about those five things. So for instance, we recently started hiring for a marketing role. And this one woman reached out to us, and she seemed great. We both spoke to her and we both liked her, and she seemed to have a lot of experience. But when she wrote to me in email, she misspelled my name, twice. And one of the five things we had decided was essential to this job was 'Attention to detail.' So in the end we decided not to hire her, because she could have easily looked up my name, and she didn't, and attention to that kind of detail was one of our 'must-haves.'"

Whatever profession or skillset you are hiring for, find out what those key questions will be. If you don't know what they are, ask someone who will know. Again, the way to get good results is to start with people you trust in your social network, and then expand from there, until you find someone who's willing to spend some time educating you about the right questions to ask and what a good answer sounds like.

Ask about everything that is hidden in silence

One vice that I see among managers who are hiring is an unwillingness to ask tough follow-up questions. If you ask a question and there is any vagueness in the answer, you need to drill down until all vagueness is eliminated and you understand exactly what the person knows. Follow up on what's said, but also follow up on what is not said.

Here's a real-life example. I asked a recent applicant (for a fullstack software job, where we were hoping to hire a novice-to-mid-level engineer):

Me: How would you improve a situation where a page is loading slowly and you suspect the problem is related to the database?

Applicant: Well, I'd start by checking the HTML, is it correctly done, and then the CSS, is there any redundancy? And then the Javascript, is it correctly written, is it minified?

Can we speed that up at all? Check the timeline, the API calls, see what is slow.

Me: Okay, great, that's a good start, but what else? If the problem is not on the frontend, then what?

Applicant: Uh, well, then, I guess I need to look at the back-end database model code. Is my database model code concise? Am I fetching the data needed, without any excess?

Me: Okay, great, that's a good start, but what else?

Applicant: Uh, what else? Well, uh, we really need to look at that database code. Is the model bloated? Can we slim it down?

Me: Yes, okay, you basically said that already, anything else?

Applicant: Uh, well ... uh, check the HTML and the CSS and the Javascript and then, uh ... API calls ... uh ... the model code, make sure that is cleaned up. That needs to be lean.

Me: Yes, okay, but you said all of that already, anything else?

Applicant: Uh ... well ... the model code ... and uh ...

Me: Have you ever worked directly with a database?

Applicant: Uh ... not much?

Me: If you get unexpected results from your model code, do you know how to debug the query?

Applicant: Uh ... I guess I could ... not really.

Me: Do you know what a Foreign Data Wrapper is in Postgres?

Applicant: Uh … no?

Me: Have you ever looked at the "slow query" log?

Applicant: Uh … no?

Me: Do you know how to run EXPLAIN or ANALYSIS?

Applicant: Well … no.

Me: Have you ever written SQL by hand?

Applicant: Uh … no.

Me: Are you aware of any differences in dialect between the SQL of MySQL and the SQL of PostGres?

Applicant: Uh … no.

Basically, they were somewhere between a novice level and a mid-level engineer, so they knew the frontend reasonably well, but they didn't know a thing about databases. Which was okay, because that was what we were looking for. We still hired them and they turned out to be great in some areas, and they were eager to learn about the things they didn't already know. But obviously, if I'd been hiring a senior-level engineer, and it turned out they knew nothing about databases, that would have been a problem. The crucial thing is that I kept asking questions until I had the full answer. Sometimes it can feel aggressive, asking the same question over and over, which can leave either you or them feeling uncomfortable. But you will never be any good at interviewing people until you learn how to tolerate uncomfortable moments.

I once shared the above story online and someone offered this criticism: "You were basically playing a game of 'Guess what I'm thinking right now' with them." But to be clear, the candidate didn't lose points because they didn't know the answer to some of my questions. I often hire novices who do not know much. I was simply trying to figure out what they knew, and what they didn't, as fast as possible. And a series of direct questions is the fastest way to figure that out.

The ultimate goal is to find out if you want to hire someone, without wasting their time or yours. Asking questions like this, directly, and digging deep, is a much faster method than handing out homework assignments and then waiting a few days for them to complete it, then reviewing it yourself, then discussing it with them. Direct, factual questions, as above, are at least as objective and as any "objective" test that you might invent.

You might ask, "But isn't this why we give written tests? To ask exactly these kinds of questions?" Yes, but when you give someone a written test, especially an online test, you won't see where they pause, where they struggle, or where they need to look something up, and so you won't know where to ask follow-up questions. Asking these questions in person allows you to focus your questions on the areas where they are struggling, so you can figure out exactly where the limits of their knowledge are.

Many managers, when they hire, don't ask tough questions either because they lack experience hiring, or because they are afraid. Thankfully, both of these shortcomings can be overcome with practice. You will get better as time goes by and hopefully, you can find ways to gain experience at this before you are the one making the decisions. Early in your career, you can certainly ask to sit in on interviews, so you can learn more about the hiring process from the manager's point of view.

Junior versus senior job candidates

When I hire junior people, I assume that I will have to invest some serious time into training them. Meaning, when I interview them, I'm less focused on how much they know, and more focused on how fast they can learn. I might give them a challenge that is beyond their skill level, and then I might offer them help. For instance, if I am hiring a software developer, I might show them some of our actual code, especially if it has a bug, and then I will ask them how to fix it. The goal is to see how well they do transforming their confusion into questions (a skill unto itself) and to see how quickly they absorb the information when I give them the answer.

When I hire senior level people, everything is the other way around: they are the teacher and I am the student. Whether I'm hiring an expert in Natural Language Processing or SEO optimization, when I hire someone senior I am hiring someone who has a speciality in which they know far more than I do. In this case the test is to find out how well they can educate me, because much of their job going forward will consist of them educating me about an aspect of the business which is crucial, and of which they are an expert.

With senior level people, a great question to ask is "Tell me about a recent project that you found difficult, but eventually you were successful." They should be excited to talk about one of their big successes, but can they translate what they know into a language that you understand? In such a situation, they are your private tutor, and you have the right to ask as many questions as you want. Drill down deep, into the details, and don't let them obfuscate any part of their project. Keep asking questions, keep drilling, until you understand what they were trying to do, what obstacles they faced, and exactly how they overcame those obstacles. They should be able to educate you right then and there; if they are unable to, then they won't be able to when you hire them. If they obfuscate their work during the job interview, they will also obfuscate their work when they have the job. When you hire someone senior, what you need to find is people who can do the work at a high level, while also explaining it to you.

Before you give someone a job offer, show them the 30 day, 60 day, and 90 day goals

Lindsey Allard is the co-founder of the very successful PlaybookUX.com. She offers this tip:

> We define the things that we want in someone, the skills that are non-negotiable. When we interview, we talk to a lot of great people, but they are not automatically the right person for the role. We might like a lot of people, but we don't try to fit a role to a person, rather, the goal is to find the person who fits the role. Even though we might like someone, if they are not the right person for that role, we don't hire them, instead we say "Well, we will stay in touch" just in case we later need someone with their skills.

> One of my big things with PlaybookUX is that we never want to hire someone, and then they start, and then they discover the job is very different than what they were expecting. In the interview process, we try to be clear, "This is exactly what you are going to be doing, here are your day-to-day activities, here are your goals." And recently, we've been creating 30 day, 60 day, and 90 day goals, and we present these to the job candidate before we give them the job offer, so they know exactly what they are getting into.

> I think too often when a company hires they focus too much on the fun stuff. They focus on the high level strategy stuff, or the creative stuff, and all of that is great, but meanwhile, they don't mention

that they also need to do data entry, and they need to review inventory, or approve invoices, and all of the other mundane stuff. So if you hire them, and they do all of these mundane activities, and six months in they have not done any high level strategy, then they are going to be upset. But we don't want them to be ambushed by the tedious side of the job, so we are upfront about that.

For a head of customer support, a 30 day goal is to be fully onboarded and able to onboard others. For a salesperson, a 30 day goal is the ability to give a demo of our software. We don't always hit our 30 day or 60 day goals, but at least we are aligned about what the job is. We set expectations upfront.

The unique difficulty of hiring great salespeople

This is, again, Lindsey Allard of PlaybookUX.com:

It can be difficult to hire great salespeople, because if someone is hitting all of their numbers, then the company, wherever they work now, is going to try really hard to hang on to them. Meaning the salespeople who are looking for jobs, a lot of them are not that great. Some of them seem really great, because they spend so much time trying to sell things, they get good at selling themselves. They present well. Sales people tend to be very confident. It can be tough to figure out who is really good.

So one thing we did was a role-play. I didn't tell them that we were going to do this, but during the last ten minutes of the interview, I'd say, okay, let's do a role-play. Totally take them off-guard. This was super helpful.

Some of the people who we really liked bombed the role-play. We asked them to do a demo for PlaybookUX. Obviously, we didn't expect them to know much about our software, but we could see if they sounded natural.

For instance, there was this one guy that I really liked, until the role-play. I introduced one scenario, where I wanted them to pretend that I was a UX researcher. I'm looking for insights into how the customers react to some UX that I've designed. That was the setup for the role play. And then I asked this candidate to sell PlaybookUX to me as if I was that researcher. They came back at me with this whole pitch about how PlaybookUX is great for marketers, and he didn't even mention research or design. And so I was thinking, okay, you didn't listen. You didn't hear me when I described who I was and what I was looking for. In a situation like that, we don't expect them to know the details of our software, because they haven't been trained yet, but we do expect them to be able to listen, and then make a pitch based on who I have described.

Some of the best people will say all of the wrong things during an interview – hire them anyway

Not everyone knows how to sell themselves. Job candidates are told to put their best foot forward, but some have no idea how to do that. In fact, some badmouth themselves, accidentally sabotaging their chances of getting a job. If you are wise, and you listen carefully, you can sometimes discover a gem that has failed most other job interviews. It is your job, as the interviewer, to discover the great talent that has been overlooked by other companies.

I'll give you an example. The year was 2006, and I lived in Charlottesville, Virginia. We needed to hire a Flash programmer. I put out a notice, got some responses, and did some interviews. I eventually found a woman, whom I'll call Lisa, who was a little less experienced than some of the other candidates, but she seemed highly motivated. She was in her early 20s and just barely out of college. Her ambition was to become a great programmer, and that came across in the projects she had done. I decided I wanted to hire her, but I had to justify the hire to Timothy, my business partner. He had veto power. We all met at the office, out in Nelson County, 45 minutes outside of Charlottesville.

When the three of us met, Timothy gave a bit of a speech about the difficulties we were facing — but also about how ambitious we were to reinvent ecommerce, especially as it related to digital goods such as songs and videos. I thought his speech was a reasonable attempt to lay out the problems we'd expect Lisa to solve.

Lisa then replied, "Yeah, I know, I'm so scared. When Lawrence offered me this job, I didn't think I could do it. I mean, it's all so complicated, and the connections to be made over the network are so uncertain, and then, everything, the timeouts, the servers, lost messages, sockets, everything I have to think about it, it's just really overwhelming and I feel scared, you know? I wasn't sure I could do it, but I guess, I don't know, maybe I should give it a try, right?"

I was astounded by this, and not in a good way. I'd been assuming that she was smart enough to know that she should put her best foot forward. And I could see the doubt on the face of my business partner. I felt I had no option except to mimic her tone and make it sound normal.

"Yes, exactly, I am so scared about all of the connections we need to make." Then I turned to Timothy. "The network can time out, the servers could jam up, the client might have a bad connection, their computer might have trouble running our frontend code — I'm definitely scared about how many obstacles we face. Lisa and I talked about this in some detail. But I'm sure we will find a solution for each of these problems."

That seemed to get us through. I managed to switch our

focus to the scary technology, which was essentially a "safer" kind of scary than hiring a woman who described herself as scared. Because talking about Lisa's fears would have been a bad way to start the relationship between her and Timothy.

We worked with Lisa for two years and we produced our biggest successes with her. She gained a lot of skill, and for as long as we relied on Flash, she was absolutely pivotal to everything we did. She eventually was worth more than we were paying her, but we had decided to move away from Flash, so we knew our relationship with her would come to an end. She got a good-paying job with the University of Virginia. In the end, the whole experience was both good for us and good for her.

Not every talented person is talented at explaining their talent

Why did Lisa almost sabotage herself at the beginning?

In the 1990s, Deborah Tannen wrote a book titled, *You Just Don't Understand: Women and Men in Conversation*. One of the points she makes is that women will often admit to a vulnerability so as to create closeness. Many female friendships start this way. Tannen makes the point that men often misread this as a lack of confidence.

My best guess is that Lisa was engaging in exactly this kind of behavior, admitting a vulnerability in an effort to start a friendship. This probably seemed natural to her. She was young enough that her social skills were still focused on the kinds of friendships she had made in college, rather than the kinds of formal relationships she would eventually make in the world of work.

But we were not her friends. We were her employers. I'm sure when she got older, she came to understand the difference. However, at that moment, she didn't understand the difference, and it almost cost her the job. Sometimes employers and employees become friends, but this should never be taken for granted.

I sometimes envy my German friends, as the ambiguity and guesswork is taken out of most social settings. The German language — like a number of others — has a formal and informal form of address, and all business relationships start with the formal form. English used to have the formal "thee" which matched the formal German "Sie," but now we only have "you" which matches the informal German "du." My friend Kristin manages an office at a farm near Dusseldorf, and it was only after three years, returning from a long illness, that the wife of the boss said to her, "I think now we should use 'du'."

In Germany one can never stupidly stumble into assuming that one's boss is a friend. It's something that is always discussed. For American workers, I would suggest that one err on the side of caution and speak in a formal manner at work until it's clear that a relationship is solid enough that one can speak more freely.

That's the advice that I would give to workers. To someone who is doing the hiring, I would suggest you keep an open mind about the different ways that people express themselves. Not every talented person is talented at explaining their talent. Some people have remarkable skills but they do a terrible job of selling themselves during job interviews. There are some absolute gems out there, people who have failed their last ten job interviews — but if you are smart you will see how talented they are, and your company will be lucky to benefit from what they can bring to the job.

Hiring leaders

When you start a company, it's just you and maybe a partner or two. If you have some success, you'll soon want to hire some help. Often, the first person you want to hire is an assistant, someone who can handle a bit of the tedious grunt work, so that you can focus on the higher-level important stuff.

The company keeps growing, and you keep hiring. At some point you try to delegate your authority over some important zone of concern and it doesn't go well. Most of your attempts at delegation go badly. You need to ask yourself: are you actually hiring leaders? Or are you still hiring assistants?

At some point, as your company expands, you need to find real leaders, people who are as competent as you are, to take over more and more of the responsibilities that are weighing you down. Sometimes you will mentor one of your assistants until they are ready to take over for you, and other times you'll hire someone new. Just keep the goal in mind: you want to find someone as intelligent and creative and driven as you are, so they can take over a zone of concern so completely that you never have to worry about it again.

For most of this chapter I talked about hiring people of junior- or mid-level skill. Hiring people at the top is both easier and more difficult: it's easier to find "social proof," as many people have worked with that job candidate over the years and can therefore comment on their strengths and weaknesses, but what you will need from them tends to be more subtle. Above all, hiring someone for a leadership position typically means that the strength of the relationship between the two of you will be more important than whatever their actual skills are. If someone is well known in the industry you can probably talk to ten different people who've worked with the person, and if those ten people all say good things about your candidate, then in some sense you know you've got someone very good, whom you probably want to hire. When you talk to them, the final question you will want to answer is whether you personally can forge a strong bond with them.

Keep in mind, you are not looking for a clone of yourself — you will not ever find a person who would do your job exactly the same way that you would do it. The person you are hiring will have their own way of getting things done, and you need to accept that as a natural part of delegating authority. What does matter is whether you feel you can speak to them with a forthright bluntness about the problems the company might face and whether they will respond with honesty. Also, if you develop unrealistic goals, do they have the integrity to push back against you?

Individuals matter

Dan Luu has written:

> One of the most common mistakes I see people make when looking at data is incorrectly using an overly simplified model. A specific variant of this, which has derailed the majority of work roadmaps I've looked at, is treating people as interchangeable, as if it doesn't matter who is doing what, as if individuals don't matter.
>
> [A] place the non-fungibility of people causes predictable problems is with how managers operate teams. Managers who want to create effective teams end up fighting the system in order to do so. Non-engineering orgs mostly treat people as fungible, and the finance org at a number of companies I've worked for forces the engineering org to treat people as fungible by requiring the org to budget in terms of headcount. The... internal bookkeeping is done in terms of "heads", so $X of budget will be, for some team, translated into something like "three staff-level heads". There's no way to convert that into "two more effective and better-paid staff level heads". If you hire two staff engineers and not a third, the "head" and the associated budget will eventually get moved somewhere else.

https://danluu.com/people-matter/

Dan Luu has written an excellent essay. This short excerpt brings up two important points to consider. First, workers are not fungible. Which leads to the second consideration: should salaries be set at the level of the corporation, or at the level of the team?

Let's tackle them in order.

Workers are not fungible

I once hired a woman who had previously been a school teacher. At the age of 30, she decided to change careers. She went to the Grace Hopper program at Fullstack Academy, which over a few months taught her the basics of computer programming. As a former teacher, she was unusually skilled at figuring out the boundary between what she knew and what she didn't. Her questions were precise, and therefore, from my perspective, it was easy to tell her exactly what she needed to know. When I interviewed her, we spoke about various frontend technologies such as React. If she knew an answer, she gave it, and if she didn't, she asked a question. She was confident enough that she did not feel any need to bluff. This already made her unique, as some job candidates feel the need to pretend they know more than they actually do.

Working with her was unusually productive, especially considering that she was at the start of her career. Her skills as a teacher constantly proved useful to the entire team. She was unusually talented at explaining her code to other people on the team, and she was able to gather up all of the confusion on the team and funnel it to me as a series of easy-to-answer questions.

I simply cannot imagine an "objective" test that could reliably reveal candidates for the artfulness with which they ask questions. It was her unique strength, and it was an important aspect of what made her successful. For as long as she was on my team, her success was also my success.

Some hiring managers will read this and respond, "That kind of unique, one-off, individual hiring doesn't scale." That may be true, but this book is mostly for entrepreneurs and managers of small- to medium-sized businesses, which are at a scale where a single bad hire can truly damage the company. Likewise, a single great hire can bring enormous benefits and enable success for such companies.

This illuminates the tension that exists between the demands from the top for legibility, versus the local knowledge that thrives and empowers each individual team. At a very large corporation, the CEO might strive to make the corporation legible to themselves by introducing standardized processes that reduce workers to fungible cogs in a great machine. But as I've said before, making a large organization legible to the person at the top often does damage to the organization. By contrast, when the top leader instead focuses on hiring great people and then delegating real authority to them, they trust that something good will come from the great people they have hired. The organization then gains a great power and a longer life.

How far can a company go when it relies on a subjective hiring process that emphasizes the complete set of factors which contribute to an individual's unique strengths? The best answer is "Go as far as you can." Hire as many people as you can on the basis of the full range of experiences that have made up their life. If, at some point, you reach a scale where the company faces criticism for a hiring process that strikes some people as arbitrary or uneven, then perhaps the company will have to adopt a standardized process. But for as long as possible, you'll want to hire individuals on the basis of their unique strengths, rather than generic bodies with some nominal functional attributes.

The crucial thing is, don't let your startup grow old prematurely. The reality of this world is simply this: workers are not fungible, and the longer you can hire unique individuals on the basis of their unique strengths, the better.

Don't Hire Candidates with Money Alone

Occasionally, I hear someone claim, "Your company should only hire the very best people!"

Beware. This is the voice of perfectionism. A small number of companies aim for elite luxury or best-in-class technology, and these companies need to aim high when hiring. However, most companies succeed with average people. They do not hire the very best people, nor pay the best salaries, nor offer the best work environment, nor produce the best product, nor create the best customer experience, nor enjoy the best margins. At best, they can offer one or two of those things. You should try to think creatively about what you can offer, when you hire.

Ideally the people who want to work with you will find some aspects of the job interesting. If the only thing you can offer is money, then you will have to pay a lot of money. But if you honestly think that you can only offer money, and nothing else, then you are probably under-selling yourself as a boss. Remember, people don't quit jobs, they quit managers. Are you the kind of manager that people hate? If not, make that clear. If other people have appreciated aspects of working with you, make that clear. Maybe you help educate people in some subject or process, or maybe you give them the time to learn something they are interested in, or maybe you occasionally introduce them to people who might be help them later in their career, or maybe you are simply known for promoting everyone who works hard, but whatever it is that you do, communicate that to people who are considering working for you.

Mark Herschberg, one of the best CTOs I ever worked with, talks about this often, and recently wrote up his advice:

You Can't Hire Candidates with Money Alone

I've been hiring tech talent for decades, beginning at the height of the dot com boom and through the years since including the hypercompetitive years of late. Having primarily worked at startups

I've always had to compete for candidates against companies in a heavier weight class. Big Tech like Amazon, Google, Facebook as well as the hot startup du jour (Uber, Twitter, Four Square) have always outclassed me when it came to cash. I learned to be effective in recruiting and closing candidates against better capitalized alternatives and you can, too.

...As I've noted in prior articles, when you compete for candidates, you are selling job openings. What do you compete on? At my startups I could not compete on salary alone (by which I mean salary, bonus, and benefits). Even throwing in stock options we weren't financially equivalent; those Big Tech companies could always outspend me. Salary matters to everyone, but it's not the only dimension. I had to be competitive with salary, but I couldn't count on being #1. (With candidates for whom salary was the only dimension, I lost out, but there was nothing I could do in those cases.)

Obviously, title / role matters as well, but presumably the candidate can find the title elsewhere. The role, however even if the same on paper, may be different from one company to the next. A vet is a vet, you take care of animals. However, working as a vet in downtown Boston is very different from working as a vet in rural Oklahoma in terms of what you're likely to encounter.

Culture, opportunity for growth, and the team (manager, peers, subordinates) are all unique. It can be similar, but is not quite the same, from one company to the next. The product / service and the mission of the company will also vary greatly.

If you're going to sell along one dimension, you better be the first choice in that dimension. Unless you're the big company in your market, odds are your salary is not the top and so you can't compete on that dimension alone.

https://www.thecareertoolkitbook.com/blog/
you-cant-hire-candidates-with-money-alone

Chapter 10

A Tale of Two Princes

In ye olde ancient days, in the kingdoms of Peridison and Katechon, the two ruling kings died in the same year, and were replaced by two young princes.

The Prince of Peridison was a bit odd, and inflicted strange rules on his court and staff. After a few years, his advisors and military leaders organized a rebellion, had the new king slain, and replaced by another. By contrast, the prince of Katechon remained popular with the court, with the advisors, the military leaders and the leading merchants, and he enjoyed a long reign.

What made them different?

The Prince of Peridison was obsessed with uniforms. On his first day he declared to the crowd assembled before him that, from that point forward, all officers of the court would have to wear a white rose, freshly picked. A few weeks later he declared they must also wear wigs made of silk. A few weeks later he declared that they must all wear boots made only of pig leather, and belts made only of beaver. Each of these new demands was an annoyance to the staff, and a minor expense, and so they were already in a bad mood when he announced he was imposing a tax on paper and ink, which angered the merchants and bookmakers. And so, when the merchants and court officers spoke, they were in agreement that the new King made arbitrary and odd decisions. Soon after, the King demanded that the navy seize a small island that had no strategic value to anyone, and the navy did so, at great expense, and to little gain. Again the King's advisors met privately and they agreed they had an unwise King who would lead the nation to ruin. When next the King began to talk of a major war against a great power, the officers of the court deposed and assassinated the King.

The prince of Katechon was more successful, though in public he seemed like an imitation of the other prince. Katechon, like Peridison, was obsessed with uniforms. He decreed that all officers of the court must wear a red rose, freshly picked. A few weeks later he declared they must wear an armband made of gold, a jacket made of mink's leather with every button made of larch wood, along with hats made of silk. The officers of the court grumbled about the large number of odd and arbitrary decisions, as well as the additional expense of these various accoutrements. A bit later, the new King of Katechon imposed a tax on paper and ink, which angered the merchants and bookmakers. Soon after, he then began talk of renewing a war with the nation's old enemy.

What gave the prince of Katechon greater success than the prince of Peridison? Everything they did in public was the same, but what they did in private was different. Whereas the prince of Peridison ignored his advisors, and only spoke to them when they were assembled as a group, the prince of Katechon spent all of his private moments talking one-on-one with the staff, and the leading citizens of the nation. When he spoke privately with his chief military general, he learned that the general's wife was sick, and so the King sent the court doctor to heal the general's wife. And when the King spoke with his chief of staff, he learned that the chief of staff had a cousin whose farm had been destroyed by devastating floods, and so the King suspended all taxes in the flooded region for two years, to allow all of the farmers in the region to recover. And when the King spoke to the nation's leading merchant, the King learned that the merchant was hoping to get his son into the nation's best university, so the

King wrote a letter of commendation that guaranteed the son would get into the best university. So, when the King considered action that some advisors viewed as dangerous, they felt they had some rapport with the King, and they could express their concerns. If the King was still set on some particular path, even after the advisor had expressed their concern, the King could depend on the advisor being loyal, even when disagreeing with the new path.

In short, one King tried to use his official power to inflict one arbitrary decree after another, upon a court and nation that had no particular reason to love or trust the king in return. The other King worked tirelessly to build goodwill with his court and with the leading citizens of the nation.

No leader has ever operated with an infinite bank of political capital. A wise leader knows that, even under the best of circumstances, one's political capital is limited, and therefore one should earn more when one can. This is a complex subject, but we can start with this simple rule: Small favors to key people is one successful strategy for building political capital.

Here is a bit of true history: in 1649, during the English Civil War, the forces loyal to Parliament captured the King and put him on trial for violating the laws of England. The King, Charles I, defended himself by saying "The law is in my mouth" meaning that since he was the King, whatever he said was automatically the law, and therefore he could never break the law. The English responded by putting him to death. Whatever the merits of his argument, he failed to address the reasons why people were angry with him. Charles I had been in power for more than 20 years, and during his reign he was very much like the prince of Peridison, always giving odd decrees, and expecting to be obeyed, while never doing anything to try to build real bonds of loyalty and affection with the key people in England.

Some people will read this parable and conclude "The only mistake made by the Prince of Peridison is that he made so many odd requests. Boots made only of pig leather, and belts made of beaver? If he hadn't made so many odd requests, then people would have trusted him more."

That is incorrect. When you are a leader, you will make many decisions, and someone in your organization will dislike your decisions and find them odd. I recently had a client where, for various complex reasons, I recommended the use of MongoDB in a situation where other consultants would probably recommend the use of Kafka, and one of the engineers reacted exactly as if I had told her that from that moment forward, she had to come to work wearing boots made only of pig leather, and belts made only of beaver. I was not able to win her over at all. But I was able to win over the rest of the engineering team. Most decisions are like that: you cannot win everyone over, but if you communicate your vision well, you can win many over. For the rest, it has to be sufficient that you've built up a bank of political capital that you can draw down when you make controversial decisions.

Where does political capital come from? That's too large a subject for this book, but we can say, simply, that it starts with one-on-one conversations. Such conversations are the most basic building block of leadership.

For other clues about leadership, there are many good books, and here I list three of my favorites:

History of the Peloponnesian War, by Thucydides.
The Prince, by Machiavelli.
Leadership in Turbulent Times, by Doris Kearns Goodwin.

Chapter 11

When companies make a fetish of being data driven, they encourage a passive-aggressive style of communication

When I talk to the 20 tech people I respect most, what I notice is that everyone esteems Google less now than five years ago. Is it a successful branding strategy which generates so much dislike?

I'm especially curious about this because Google is famous for basing its decisions on "data." In terms of what people do online, no one has more data than Google, so of course it makes sense that it uses data to make decisions. And thanks to this brilliant strategy of using data … uh … well … Google hasn't launched a successful product since 2008.

Google launched their search engine in 1998, Gmail in 2004, and Google Maps in 2005. They bought YouTube in 2005. In 2006, they launched an office product (documents and spreadsheets). In 2008, they launched the Android operating system for mobile phones, which gained massive worldwide market share. Since then, they haven't had many successful products they can point to.

They built a great RSS reader, called Google Reader, which users loved — but management eventually felt it was too much of a niche product, so they got rid of it. In 2006 they launched Google Pages, which made it easy for people to create their own websites, but again, it was considered too niche so eventually they shut it down (they could have dominated the space that is now divided up among SquareSpace, Wix, and WordPress, but they walked away from all of it). In 2002 they had purchased Picasa, which many people loved for organizing the photos on their computers, but Google got bored and canned it in 2011.

Of all of Google's failures, the most infamous is Google+, the social network that was supposed to crush Facebook. Sadly, Google+ never gained traction. Despite absolutely massive amounts of data about what people supposedly want to do on-line, and despite the benefit of a ridiculously huge marketing budget, Google could not design a social network that anyone wanted to use. Depending on which starting point you accept, it was launched in either 2011 or 2015, and then shut down in 2019. This was a data-driven failure on a grand scale.

But without question, the longest and most consistent string of failures at Google involves online chat, especially video. On this subject, Google is looking back at 15 years during which they have failed to come up with a consistent branding for their chat experience. For instance, Meebo was a chat company, founded in 2005, which became very popular — and it was bought by Google in 2012, yet Google killed it by folding it into its doomed Google+ social network.

Consider Google Spaces. Oh, wait, you've never heard of it? That's an interesting coincidence, because no one else has ever heard of it either. You'd think a company that practically has a monopoly on Web search might be able to make more people aware of one of its newest attempts at chat. Google Spaces launched in 2016 and was shut down in 2017, which really makes me wonder how a company with so much data can demonstrate such little confidence in its ability to iterate on a product and eventually make it successful. (Google Spaces was supposed to compete with Slack, but Slack remains the most popular chat platform.)

Consider, also, all Google's attempts at branding it:

- Google Talk
- Google Wave
- Google Hangouts
- Google Meetings
- Duo
- Allo

The video service has repeatedly been folded into the work product, which was called Google Apps and then Google G-suite and then Google Workspace.

A basic video service is easy to set up, and Yahoo offered a great one back in 2004. In fact, when Laura Denyes and I set up our own web design company in 2007, we were often in different cities — so we would turn on Yahoo video and leave it on for 12 hours, the whole entire time we were working. We'd literally just leave it open on our computers so that every time we looked up we'd see each other, which was as good as being in the same room with the other person.

What's difficult about chat or video is figuring out how to monetize it. Precisely because it is so easy to set up, there will always be many such services that are free — so how can a company make any money from it? Slack is now the most popular chat service for teams, but its revenues are limited because its basic product is free. A company only has to pay for Slack if they want admin controls and archives.

Despite a massive amount of data, Google cannot figure out a way to monetize video chat. It is simply amazing that Slack was able to come out of nowhere, around the time that Google was failing with Google Spaces and Google+, and win the market share that Google wanted but didn't know how to get. This suggests that intuition sometimes beats data — and the folks at

Slack had the right intuition. But let's also consider, were there other reasons why Google was unable to take advantage of the massive amounts of data that it had?

When the leadership doesn't like the data: Tumblr is important to the international community of gays, lesbians, and trans individuals

Marissa Mayer was employee number 20 at Google, and for years she led usability and product development. She was a loud advocate of data-driven decision making. And yet, what did that gain her? In 2012 she left Google and became CEO of Yahoo. The tech industry wondered, could data-driven decisions save Yahoo? The results offer a clear "no." Yahoo continued down-hill and in 2017 it was sold to Verizon, at which point Mayer left the company.

Let's consider one particular mistake. In 2013, Yahoo acquired Tumblr for $1.1 billion. In 2019, Verizon sold it for just above $0. That's $1.1 billion of value that was wiped out thanks to Mayer. Yet she was making these data-driven decisions, so what exactly went wrong?

Tumblr is important to the international LGBT community. Anyone who has spent even ten minutes on Tumblr is aware that it is full of gay, queer, and trans content. Did Mayer realize that when she bought it? Was she amenable to it? Under her leadership there were several attempts to remove some of the porn from Tumblr, but the crackdown was overly broad and swept away a large amount of non-explicit LGBT content, which understandably outraged gay activists all over the world. A permanent animosity developed between the most active users of Tumblr and its owners.

When you consider this situation, also consider the counter-factual: what might have happened if Tumblr had come under the leadership of someone who loved all of the fandoms, rejoiced in the idiosyncrasies of the sub-cultures, and celebrated the intensity with which users engaged in the shared material? Tumblr was, and is, blessed with a large user base that is fanatical in its devotion to the community that exists thanks to the site. With the right leadership, could some of that $1 billion have been saved?

One of the many limits to data-driven decision making is when the leadership simply has no affinity for the customer base. No amount of data will fix that.

Data isn't a cure for overconfidence; rather, data can make overconfidence worse

I don't mean to just pick on Google and its alumni. Consider Steve Ballmer, who joined Microsoft in 1980, became CEO in 2000, gained complete control of the company when Bill Gates retired in 2006, and then ran it until 2014. Although Ballmer also spoke of the importance of making data-driven decisions, his 14 years as CEO are generally seen as a long period of stagnation for Microsoft. After all, what did the data tell Ballmer? It told him that Windows was important to Microsoft profits, therefore he kept the whole company focused on Windows. This meant that Microsoft missed out on the transition to the cloud, as well as the arrival and explosive growth of smartphones, after the iPhone was introduced in 2007.

Data is often retrospective. You will have data about the huge profits your old products made last year, but you won't have data about the profits your newest product will make five years in the future.

Perhaps most importantly, data doesn't save you from disaster. For instance, the home-buying website Zillow has more information about home prices than anyone else, yet they just made this announcement in November 2021:

> CEO Rich Barton now says that "We've determined the unpredictability in forecasting home prices far exceeds what we anticipated and continuing to scale Zillow Offers would result in too much earnings and balance-sheet volatility." With the program shutting down, the company says it's reducing the estimated value of the houses it purchased in Q3 or will purchase in Q4 by more than $500 million. Zillow also says that winding down the business in the coming months will mean having to let go of almost 25 percent of its employees — almost 2,000 workers.
>
> https://www.theverge.com/2021/11/2/22760080/zillow-of-fers-home-selling-ibuyer-wind-down-excess-inventory-losses-financial-results

I've met leaders who cling to reports full of statistics the way toddlers cling to a security blanket, yet the statistics don't actually protect them from the vagaries of life. To be clear, my message here is not anti-intellectual. I think you should strive to be as well-informed as possible. But in the end, you'll have to make decisions without knowing all of the information that might be useful to you. That is true both in life and in business, of course; none of us knows what tomorrow will bring.

At a big company, like Google or Microsoft, data is simply going to tell you that your old products make a lot of money but your new products don't make much money. In other words, the data is just telling you something stupidly obvious: that your new products are still small. This is about as insightful as saying the sun rises in the east. Your 10 year-old product will be making billions while the product you introduced last month is only making a few million. So if you want to make data-driven decisions, obviously you should shut down all of your new products and remain loyal to your oldest products? But wait, isn't there a risk that your oldest products will someday be too old? If you give the most resources to your biggest products, you'll end up defending the past instead of inventing the future.

In short, having a lot of data doesn't save you from the need to use wisdom, intuition, reasonableness, and proportionality when deciding what to do.

A master craftsman will have intuitions about their craft which they won't be able to explain to you

Most successful product launches are overseen by someone who is deeply committed to getting that product off the ground. That person will have devoted years of their life to understanding the customer who needs and wants that particular product. The person overseeing that product launch will eventually build up dozens of important intuitions which can be difficult to verbalize in a language that the CEO will understand (likewise, an entrepreneur launching their own startup will often have trouble explaining to investors exactly why customers love a given product). If "data-driven decision making" refers to careful studies of massive sets of user statistics, then data-driven decision making can never function correctly for truly innovative new products, as there simply won't be enough data for the CEO to study.

This point is subtle and easily misunderstood: entrepreneurs and product managers will spend a great deal of time talking to customers and thus gaining data and insights into what the customers actually want. Yet this kind of soft, tacit knowledge is not what is typically meant when CEOs talk about data-driven decision making.

A great designer will crave data and try to get as much as possible: ethnographic studies, customer interviews, formal A/B testing at sufficient scale to rule out statistical anomalies, simple multiple-choice surveys, heat-map studies to show usage patterns, and so much more. A master of user experience (UX) is always looking for new tools and methods to help them get more insights about the customer. This expert will then combine that data with everything they've learned over the course of their career, and they will synthesize all of it to a few intuitions that will guide their work. They may have trouble verbalizing the process by which their intuitions are derived, but the correctness of those intuitions should be deducible from the final result: are customers happy?

In other words, the correct place for data-driven decision making to happen is inside the mind of the talented experts that you have hired. Such people use a lot of data to form their opinions. Once they give you their opinion, there is no need to re-hash the data behind that opinion. Having a large, raucous meeting where people quote statistics at each other can only undermine, and never enhance, the expertise of the professionals that you've hired.

As far as I know, there has never been a company that said, "We want the worst informed, most ignorant people to make the decisions," so in a sense, all companies have always valued data. They just didn't make a fetish out of it. They simply expected people to be well informed and to make intelligent arguments, based on what they knew. That would have been true at General Motors in 1950 at least as much as at Google in 2015. Indeed, this much has probably been true at most companies for centuries. When management says that the company is going to be "data-driven," they are implicitly asking for a particular type of interaction to happen in meetings, an elaborate dance where people pantomime the objectivity of scientists while still relying on the implicit knowledge they've gained over the many years of their career.

The more emphasis given to certain metrics, the more employees will manipulate that metric

As soon as the leadership agrees that certain metrics are the crucial ones for measuring success, there is the risk that employees will manage the metric itself, instead of the underlying reality. As Page Laubheimer and Kate Moran have written:

> One of the most misquoted sayings in business is "if you can't measure it, you can't manage it." This statement (and its variations) is often meant to say that, to improve something, we need a precise metric that captures it and that should be tracked in order to understand if our efforts to improve it are effective.

> It is interesting that this "quote" is actually the complete opposite of the original, which was:

> *"It is wrong to suppose that if you can't measure it, you can't manage it – a costly myth."* — W. Edwards Deming (The New Economics, 1993).

> This difference between the original and the commonly used version highlights why it's dangerous to rely on a single metric to assess how well a business is performing: that one metric can be manipulated in ways unrelated to what it is supposed to measure. This is the phenomenon described by Campbell's law.

> Campbell's law states that the more important a metric is in social decision making, the more likely it is to be manipulated.

> In other words, when a single metric is used to determine success or failure, human beings are likely to try to optimize their behavior to improve that metric — sometimes with ridiculous or dangerous consequences. People manage the metric, rather than using the metric to help manage the underlying issue of interest. ...

> A metric is a signal that reflects the goal or outcome you're seeking,

but is not the full picture. There is no one truly absolute metric that completely captures a real-world behavior or phenomenon. Just because a measure is quantitative, does not mean that the data collected will be free from bias.

https://www.nngroup.com/articles/campbells-law/

An example of this happened at GE at the end of the 1980s. Jack Welch was the CEO and he introduced email in the hopes it would allow managers to make faster decisions with better communication. However, the executives stuck to their old habits: they would carefully dictate a memo to their secretary, the secretary would then read it back to the executive, the executive would then direct the secretary to make certain edits. The only difference is that these well-crafted memos were now sent as email instead of being sent on paper. Welch became frustrated with this and told his executives that they were missing out on the fast-paced, improvisational kind of idea generation that they could now do, thanks to the speed of email. He demanded that they write less carefully and more authentically. Where, he asked, were the typos? If they were really writing in an improvisational way, their emails would be full of typos. At that point, the executives adopted a new style for writing memos: they would carefully dictate a memo to their secretary, the secretary would then read it back to the executive, the executive would then direct the secretary to make certain edits, and then the final step was to go back through and add in some typos. As soon as Welch suggested that the number of typos was a new mark of quality, his executives became strategic about adding in some typos.

Trust your instincts and your team, not your ego

I recommend this to all professionals. Over the years, we often condense many years of learning to a few simple rules. If you asked me from what peer-reviewed study I learned to value minimalist design for software, I would not be able to answer you. It comes from dozens of books, hundreds of articles, thousands of conversations, and countless observations — and if the accumulated wisdom of my years of experience is of no value to you, then why did you hire me?

To the entrepreneurs who are running a startup, I would say the same: hire good people and then trust them. Do not force them to use a style of communication that might not be natural for them. Do not ask them to pretend that their subtle, tacit, implicit insights and intuitions can be reduced to a few statistics that they can then use to make their knowledge explicit for you. You need to accept that they will always know things that you will not know. They cannot take a lifetime of experiences and make all of it legible to you; that is simply not a reasonable thing to expect, whether in a professional setting or a personal one.

The opposite of abusive leadership isn't bland leadership; it's respectful leadership

When I criticize meetings which force participants to behave in a "data-driven" style, I mean that experts should instead be allowed to speak in a manner which they themselves find natural. I am not advocating for unprofessional behavior, and I'm certainly not saying that people should feel free to vent their feelings when they are feeling anger. No one in a professional setting should be disrespected or disrespectful. But hopefully everyone can see, the opposite of an abusive meeting is not a bland meeting in which people quote meaningless statistics. Rather, the opposite of an abusive meeting is one where people listen respectfully to experts who have many insights to share, thanks to their years of experience.

What is "data-driven decision making" a euphemism for? Mostly it's meant to indicate the opposite of ego-driven decision making. A company that advertises that it makes decisions based on data is trying to indicate that it doesn't allow top leaders to scream, throw things, sexually harass underlings, or treat their every impulse as a sacred edict. Over the last few years, as cases of abuse have gotten more and more public attention, and the MeToo movement has gained more attention, it's become clear that many companies have previously allowed a dysfunctional style of leadership. It is altogether appropriate to build a movement to ensure that leadership is going to reform itself. Making calm decisions based on a stack of statistics is clearly better than making decisions based on ego and impulse. But neither of these options is ideal. We should always be clear about what is ideal: hire good people, listen to them with proper care and diligence, respect what they know – *all* that they know, both the implicit and explicit.

Do not let stacks of data ever give you the impression that somewhere out there is some expert that will always have the right answers. Given a truly novel situation, or a truly original technology, thick reports full of statistics and even expert intuitions will all have limited value. When you're rafting through the most tumultuous of the white waters, the most important resource you can have is the trust that exists amongst the members of your team. A trust that is nurtured and strengthened by small group or one-on-one meetings. No amount of data can replace that.

Chapter 12

A blind commitment to flatness damages your organization

Over the last 15 or 20 years, one vice that's become popular among Silicon Valley types is a fetish for "flat organizations." Supposedly these will save us from the horrors of bureaucracy. Obviously every organization should want to remain as flat as possible, and you shouldn't take on extra expenses for no reason. But you need to look at this issue pragmatically, not theoretically.

There are multiple ways that a rigid commitment to flatness damages your organization:

1. Each top leader (because even "flat organizations" typically still have a CEO, a CTO, a CFO, and perhaps a CMO) will have so many direct reports that as a practical matter they are no longer really leaders. They become symbolic figureheads who no longer know what their team is doing. Any leader with more than 20 people who talk to them directly is likely stretched thin, overworked, and unable to follow up on important initiatives. They might boast that they've avoided the vice of micromanaging, which is

true, but they've gone to the other extreme and large-ly shirked their responsibilities.

2. Flatness is unfair to the most experienced people on the teams. A good friend of mine was, for all practical purposes, the head of devops at a very large analytics firm, and he had to architect an ambitious system for consuming and processing a terabyte of data a day. But he can't put "Head of devops" on his resume because such titles didn't exist at his company. The organization's strict commitment to flatness robbed him of the recognition (and pay) that he deserved.

3. Ironically, one still ends up with the worst kind of micromanagement. Regarding the friend I just men-tioned, in theory everyone on the devops team was equal, no matter how much experience they had — so when there was a dispute, he couldn't simply resolve the issue. He wasn't the team leader because there *were* no team leaders. Every disagreement had to be taken to the CTO. In such a situation, the CTO will tend to be poorly informed on most issues, as there are too many issues for any one person to keep track of. If there had been a "frontend team leader" and "database team leader" and "devops team leader" then most disputes could be resolved at a lower level, but creating such mid-level managers would create hierarchy. Yet without them, every heated argument percolates up to the top.

Do you want every decision to go to the top?

Some of the advocates of flat organizations have said to me, "So long as everyone acts like a real adult and talks things over with real maturity, then the teams can resolve disputes on their own, without having to take their issues to the very top."

I suspect that such advocates are subconsciously thinking of family dynamics: if children could act like real adults, then they wouldn't have to take their disputes to the parents. But that assumes the fight is over something trivial, like toys or clothes or video games. Among professionals, the issues will often be over strategic initiatives, where two options are both valid but each commits the company to a different path. A question like, "Should the database team use a distributed, high write-volume NoSQL database, or a traditional database with a RabbitMQ queue in front of it?" is not like two children arguing over a toy. Strong arguments can be made for either option, but it is a major architectural decision and it will shape how software is developed at the company for many years to come. "Act like an adult" also means "defend your professional opinion based on all you've learned over the course of your whole career," which doesn't exactly lend itself to compromise on important issues. But somewhere in the system there has to be a leader who can make a choice and then accept all the consequences and responsibilities of having made that choice. So the only real question is, will your company empower mid-level managers to make those decisions, or will every decision be brought all the way to the top?

As a point of contrast, remember Eric Garside at Freshly. Recall that he had 15 direct reports when the team had 30 people; that's 15 people he was trusting to make most day-to-day decisions so he didn't have to think about them. Later, when he needed even more distance from the inner workings of the tech team, he elevated his two most trusted lieutenants and left nearly all the work to them. By all accounts, Garside managed this transition in a pragmatic fashion, without any rigidness about keeping the organization flat nor any particular desire to make it more hierarchical. He simply did what he deemed best for the company. It wasn't a political question for him, it was common sense.

You cannot build a vibrant, successful organization if you try to follow simplistic slogans such as, "All bureaucracy is bad." Nor is it valid to say, "All bureaucracy is good." The only appropriate approach is to figure this out empirically. Remember, this isn't a political question, this is an issue for pragmatism.

Depending on how fast you are growing, you might need to hire managers in excess of what you currently need. Peter Drucker, when he was working as a consultant, would ask CEOs, "How would your organization be able to react if a big sale came in that doubled your sales?" If the CEO responded, "Well, of course we'd be happy for the new business but, wow, it would be a burden to try to meet that big a spike in demand," then Drucker would answer, "You're too lean. You need to start hiring and training more managers right now."

Put another way: if running a "flat organization" means that all of your top leaders have to work 60 hours a week to keep up with their many direct reports, then your organization is brittle and cannot react quickly to changing circumstances, because your leadership is already spread thin and exhausted. Likewise, if your top leadership only works 40 hours a week but is ignoring most of their direct reports, then your organization is, very simply, poorly organized and poorly led.

But won't bureaucracy ruin our company?

Don't ever think that a badly functioning bureaucracy is the natural state of bureaucracies. That is a fatal assumption.

As customers and as citizens, all of us have had a few bad experiences with bureaucracies run amok. You call your cable company and tell them you want to cancel your account, but a month later you are still billed for the service. In government, sometimes a rogue agency gains too much autonomy and starts granting itself a larger budget, feeding its own growth like a cancer and unaccountable to the public. So too, with some police forces, which often have more power than the civilians who are elected to oversee them.

So we know, bureaucracies *can* be bad – but do they have to be? Aren't they also a stabilizing force in an organization? Once you are in charge of building your own bureaucracy, you need to commit to doing it right. Don't run away from the difficulties, but rather, face them head on. Is it difficult to design a truly beautiful architecture for your bureaucracy? Yes, it is at least as difficult as designing a truly beautiful architecture for a large software system. But it can be done, and you'll need to do it if you want your business to grow beyond a certain point.

Take, for instance, money. A small team of highly ethical individuals can generally trust one another to safeguard money in an appropriate way. Many small churches and family businesses are run this way, with loose controls over who can deposit or spend. However, as a company grows, the chance you'll hire an unethical individual also grows. At a certain scale it is almost certain that a worker will steal some money, if they have the chance to do so. So a company must impose rules about handling money, and there needs to be a process for paying bills, with someone authorized to write checks and use the company credit cards. This is the beginning of your financial bureaucracy, and the tight limit on who holds the authority to spend is the beginning of hierarchy in this area.

Is this a bad thing? Again, you'll confuse yourself if you think about this in terms of good or bad. Just focus on your goals. What strengths do you want to build into your organization?

Nowadays, there is a widespread idea that bureaucracy makes an organization rigid. But consider the ways that a well-designed bureaucracy for money control can make your organization more flexible. If you decide to keep your money-control bureaucracy small then you'll also need to keep your purchasing process simple, perhaps by centralizing all purchasing decisions in the hands of the CEO or CFO. That one individual then becomes a choke point that limits progress; nothing can get done until they find time to pay some bills and buy some necessary materials or services. There is an obvious limit on how much the company can grow when the authority to pay a bill is so limited. Yet, even when the money handling bureaucracy grows to three or four people, that still might not be enough to oversee complex spending patterns, so your company will be forced to follow simple and inflexible rules. By contrast, what if you wanted to decentralize the power to make purchases? What if you wanted to empower each team with the ability to make whatever purchases they felt they needed, up to some reasonable limit? That would make your organization much more flexible, but it also makes it more difficult to track the money, and therefore it requires a larger bureaucracy for tracking each dollar. The point is, the larger bureaucracy can actually help enable some kinds of decentralized decision making, and thus improve the agility of the organization. A growing bureaucracy does not automatically equal growing inflexibility. Rather, the whole point is to try to maintain flexibility at scale.

When I've said this to entrepreneurs, many of them respond with "Well, what about _____ ," and then they mention some famously terrible bureaucracy that hurt people while consuming enormous amounts of money. And my response is always the same: "Yes, that bureaucracy really sucked. Don't build anything like that. Build something better. If you want to grow, then you've got no option except to build a bureaucracy, so you should have the ambition to build a great one."

Should salaries be set at the level of the corporation, or at the level of the team?

If you've read my book, *How to Destroy a Tech Startup in Three Easy Steps*, then you know how much I pleaded for a better NLP expert (that is, a software developer who understood the techniques of Natural Language Processing) at the startup where I worked in 2015. The person who had been hired for this position had proven himself incompetent, and when I inquired why he was kept on staff, I was told, "He's willing to work for a below-average salary." But he wasn't able to do the work, so he was still too expensive for what we got from him.

As Dan Luu says, there are times when a team can go faster with two excellent people than with three average people. Is it possible to pay those two people 50% more, that is, the money that would have gone to the third person?

In some companies, the Human Resources department defines all jobs and defines what salaries can be paid for each job. Organizing head count this way, and salaries this way, helps to make the organization legible to the top leadership. However, it imposes limits on whom the organization can hire.

Can a team leader simply be given control over a big lump of money and then empowered to spend that money as they see fit? In that scenario, the team leader can decide whether it is best to hire three average people or two extraordinary people.

Again, there are no strategies that work for every company in every situation. But this is a strategy worth considering. Keep in mind the accounting becomes more difficult when the power to create salaries or make purchases is pushed out to individual teams.

In 1986 Bill Gates, who was the CEO of Microsoft, was attending a technology conference when the CEO of an office supply vendor came up to him and said, "What's wrong with you people? Why won't you pay your bills? You're more than four months delinquent on the invoices I've been sending you. I thought you were doing well. Are you secretly bankrupt?"

Gates was shocked. Microsoft was flush with cash and could easily pay the invoices, but no one in the accounting office knew who this vendor was. Microsoft had decentralized buying decisions to the individual teams, but the accounting was still centralized, because setting up an independent accounting department for every team would have been wasteful and redundant. So what had happened was that some team had bought supplies from this vendor, but when the accounting department got the invoice, they couldn't match it to any actual purchase. They thought it was a scam, so they didn't pay the bill. That is, there had been a breakdown in communication between teams that made the purchase and the accounting team that had to pay the bill. (See *Hard Drive: Bill Gates and the Making of the Microsoft Empire*, by James Wallace and Jim Erickson.)

In the end, this wasn't a serious issue. Gates personally authorized the invoices and got them paid, and changes were made in the way that the individual teams communicated their purchasing decisions back to the central accounting department. A mere bump in the road, the kind of growing pains every organization goes through as it transforms from a small company into a big company. Microsoft gained a lot of advantages by empowering individual teams to make their own purchasing decisions. For instance, the teams with software developers could buy custom computers, much more powerful than what was needed by the average office worker — and the design teams could modernize their workflows without having to constantly plead with the central office over each purchase.

It is possible to leave budget decisions to individual teams. It takes a bit of extra work to get the accounting right, but it can be done, and it imparts an important flexibility to the organization. However, if you want to push this kind of decision making power down to the level of the teams, don't be afraid of the fact that it takes a bit of extra bureaucracy to keep track of everything. It's a bit of a paradox, but sometimes more bureaucracy allows more decentralization. That's especially true when it comes to dispersing money, while keeping track of it.

When you do introduce hierarchy, be sure authority goes with responsibility

In contrast to the previous examples, and at the other extreme, I have consulted with a few companies who had people who were called "managers" and yet they had no real power. Whenever they were asked to make a decision, they had to ask permission from their manager, and sometimes that manager had to ask permission from their manager. These were organizations that achieved the worst of all possible worlds: they were highly hierarchical, with multiple levels of management, but still, every decision had to go to the top, just like the worst examples of the extremely flat organizations.

The general rule to follow is this: each person should have the authority to carry out their responsibilities. There is something almost cruel, and certainly inefficient, when you give someone a responsibility, but then you don't give them the authority to fulfill that responsibility. If you've made someone the leader of a team, they should have the power to make all of the decisions that are local to that team.

In conclusion, don't make a fetish out of flatness. Rather, you need to react to reality. Delegate your authority when you can, understanding that delegation introduces hierarchy. Always be pragmatic about this, balancing the cost of having more managers with the benefits of delegating your authority over some area (budget, marketing, inventory, design, tech) so that you no longer have to worry about that area. And when you delegate, really delegate; don't create false managers who have responsibilities but no power.

In the next example, we'll take a look at what happens when one-on-one meetings are not used, but should be.

Chapter 13

When everything goes wrong: what the absence of one-on-one meetings looks like

Unfortunately, I have often seen top leaders engage in one-on-one conversations while in the middle of a large group meeting. There might be fourteen people in the room, but all of the conversation is between the leader and one other person. I find it amazing when the leader either lacks the self-awareness to see what they are doing or has so much ego that they don't mind wasting the time of the dozen people who are sitting there as unhappy spectators.

Case Study: Open Verse Media

When I first started at Open Verse Media, an ebook publisher, they asked me to look at their content management system (CMS/CRM). The staff had to rely on it, but it was very slow. The COO, whom I'll call Robin, had overseen the creation of this app. The actual work of creating the software was outsourced to one firm, but after two years Robin felt they were too expensive. She fired that first firm and then hired a firm in Ohio, which I'll call MegaStars.

The app had been built using a popular software framework called Ruby On Rails. Whenever Robin felt that a new feature was needed, she would ask MegaStars to add the feature. MegaStars billed $500 an hour, and over the course of seven years, a total of $3 million had been spent on the creation of this app.

The staff hated the app. When the head of marketing wanted to bring up the top 100 best-selling books, they would click on a link, and it would take a full 60 seconds for the page to come up. The staff had gotten used to the fact that they always needed to be engaged in two tasks, that is, something to keep them busy while they waited for the pages in the CMS to render. An advanced search, with multiple filters, could take up to five minutes to render a report. Many of the lower-level staff would simply go into Slack and engage in gossip with their peers while waiting for each page to slowly appear.

So on my first day I logged into our main web server, and right away I could see that the app was generating several thousand errors each hour, all of which were being written to a log file. Since this app was single-threaded, the work of writing the errors to the log file had to happen while each page was rendering. This was one major reason why it was so slow.

This arms-length relationship needed to be closer.

Why did this app have so many problems? Well, when Robin requested a new feature, MegaStars would tell her exactly how much time was needed to get that feature done. If they felt a new feature needed 30 hours to build, they would simply quote $15,000 as the price tag. Sometimes the new work conflicted with old work and generated new problems, but that wasn't in the estimate and therefore the new problems needed to be ignored as much as possible. This tactic of ignoring new problems had been going on for many years. Additionally, much of the code base was now out of date and suffered version conflicts whenever some parts of the system needed to use newer libraries of code (which in Ruby On Rails are called "gems").

MegaStars could have said, "Pay us $100,000 and we will clean up all of these problems." But then Robin might ask, "Why did you allow these problems to exist? What are we paying you for?" It might seem like a scam, if MegaStars asked for more money to fix the problems that they themselves had created.

Here was the central dynamic of the situation: Robin felt she held power because she could terminate the relationship at any time. In fact, all of the problems in the relationship were because she could end the relationship at any time and was leaning on that fact as her main way of getting compliance. MegaStars was unwilling to commit to the long-term health of the software while Robin was constantly threatening to fire them.

Any code base will develop some "tech debt," that is, mistakes which need to be carefully refactored out of the code. When you have full-time software developers on your staff, or a long-term, trusting relationship with an outside team, they often feel a sense of ownership regarding the code they are creating. Like great craftspeople, they take pride in their work. They will want to resolve any ugliness in the code as soon as possible.

Tech debt tends to accumulate when software developers are facing a deadline. The developers get sloppy and cut some corners. After the deadline has been met, then they can go back and clean up the code. After all, when they have a long-term commitment to the code, they want it to be of high quality.

When you work with an outside agency, they typically can't or won't go back and clean up the code, because the customer is not willing to pay $500 an hour for that work. Some of the better agencies try to include the clean-up work in the overall price, but then those agencies seem expensive — and they get undercut by other agencies that are willing to do the absolute minimum, even if that means writing poor-quality code full of errors.

More one-on-one meetings would have helped

In many ways, the situation was worse than what I've already described. "Robin asked MegaStars to add a new feature" – what does this really mean? As a practical matter, the real process was something like this:

1. The staff hated the CMS.

2. Occasionally the frustration was so intense that it bubbled up to Robin.

3. Robin would convene a large meeting, including all team leads and their assistants.

4. Robin would give a speech emphasizing the need to control the budget, plus various warnings she had received from MegaStars – without doing a full re-write, MegaStars felt there was a limited amount they could do. Plus a full re-write would be too expensive.

5. Then Robin opened the floor to suggestions.

6. Everyone threw out some ideas, but without any knowledge of how much a feature might cost, and no real idea of what the budget was, the staff tended to engage in self-censorship.

7. Robin would pick three or four ideas that seemed interesting, then send them in written form to MegaStars.

8. MegaStars would send back a cost estimate.

9. Robin would then approve whatever items she felt were within the budget.

10. A new contract would be signed between Robin and MegaStars, regarding the next batch of work.

11. MegaStars would deliver the work, but without cleaning up some of the long-standing problems.

Please note, this is not a rant about out-sourcing. I've seen companies have great results while working with an outside agency. The real issue is this: if your company depends on an outside relationship, then that relationship needs to be a close, long-term, trusting relationship.

There were several factors that caused things to get so bad at Open Verse:

1. The CEO was an industry legend, but rather elderly, so she pushed most of her responsibilities onto her COO. Robin was therefore spread thin with too many responsibilities.

2. The CEO and COO had spent much of their careers in print publishing, and were slow to realize how different ebooks were. (Books that sold well were more topical, less based on the prestige of the writer.)

3. Robin was very slow to realize how much the organization depended on the CMS. She herself didn't use it, so perhaps she didn't realize how painful it was for staff to have to wait 60 seconds for a page to render.

4. Robin thought her power, regarding MegaStars, lay in the fact that she could fire them. In fact, this was a source of weakness in the relationship.

It does not matter if your company has an internal tech team or works with an external agency, if you are the COO, be prepared to have long one-on-one conversations with whoever is heading up your software development. Obviously the COO is going to push day-to-day management of the tech team to someone else (a CTO or a project manager who can operate at a high level) but then the COO needs to be in frequent contact with that person.

Who should accumulate requests for new features in the software? That should be the CTO or project manager, not the

COO. It should be a regular, on-going process, not an occasional ad-hoc event. It needs to be someone who has the time to sit with those making the requests, talk to them one-on-one, and translate what they claim to need into what they really need.

One way or another, the only path forward for Open Verse Media was to find someone who could manage the software on a day-to-day basis. There were two possibilities:

1. Hire a project manager and let her manage the relationship with the outside agency. The project manager could focus on building a close, trusting relationship with that agency.

1. Hire a CTO, plus several software developers, and bring all software development in house.

Open Verse Media decided to go with the latter option. They fired MegaStars and instead hired a CTO plus several software developers. This should have given Open Verse Media the ability to move forward with faster and better software, as well as the ability to imagine software projects much more ambitious than anything that had been possible in the awkward and distrustful relationship with MegaStars.

As it happened, Open Verse Media hired the wrong person to be CTO. This person was an egomaniac and very controlling. This irritated the software developers, and after eight months there was a mass exodus where the whole tech team quit. If the goal was to get a team that could care about the software over the long-term, choosing the wrong person to be the team leader undermined the intent — a fact that keeps us from drawing any easy or simple conclusions from this story, regarding the benefits of out-sourcing versus in-sourcing. It evidently isn't true that bringing the work in-house ensures the project will go smoothly. There remain other factors that can sabotage the situation. However, the fact remains that the relationship between the COO and MegaStars was unable to be productive because of distrust between the parties.

A final point: when I say a long-term trusting relationship is needed regarding any technology or role that is essential to the survival of the business, some people mistakenly think I mean that you should trust blindly. I actually mean the opposite: fire anyone you don't trust, and fire them quickly. Above I said wrote "Robin felt she held power because she could terminate the relationship at any time. In fact, all of the problems in the relationship were because she could end the relationship at any time and was leaning on that fact as her main way of getting compliance." My point is, if she had doubts about MegaStars, then she should have fired them quickly and then found someone else she could trust. Her mistake was in constantly making the threat of firing them, without ever actually firing them. Her constant threats left the relationship ambiguous and distrustful, precisely the thing you need to avoid when dealing with the people (whether internal or external) who create the software that the whole company depends on.

Chapter 14

Dreaming of a perfect future versus a pragmatic focus on the present

In this chapter I tell two stories of success and two stories of failure. With both of the entrepreneurs who failed, the failure was completely self-inflicted. This is a sadly common story: these entrepreneurs had the chance to become fantastically wealthy, but they sabotaged themselves. A bit more self-awareness, a bit more self-honesty, a willingness to confront their own insecurities: that was all they needed to become successful. But they got lost in daydreams about how great the future would be, and they spent more and more time daydreaming the more they realized how much they were ruining the present. By contrast, the two success stories that I here tell had a simple habit that lead to success, and then to even more success: they stayed focus on what they could do right now.

Every entrepreneur fears failure; that is totally normal. The difference between success and failure is how they deal with that fear. If you're not constantly talking to customers, trying to build a startup is like trying to hike to the top of a melting glacier. For a while you think you're making progress, but then you slide all the way back down to the beginning. Showing your product or service to people helps ground your sense of progress in reality. Otherwise your fears can completely cloud your judgment.

Some entrepreneurs resist showing their progress because they are worried that showing a half-built product will leave potential customers with a bad first impression. There are some industries, especially anything to do with luxury and glamor, where making a good first impression is essential. In such cases, it's crucial to find the best possible proxy for real customers. Typically, success in such industries is led by someone who has been in the industry a long time and has therefore built up a familiarity about what the customer wants. The important thing is to have some way to ground your beliefs in reality so you don't get caught in a cycle of guessing. Guessing will lead to doubts which can then spiral all the way to paranoia.

As I wrote about in my book, *How to Destroy a Tech Startup in Three Easy Steps*, in 2015 I worked with a startup that wanted to use Natural Language Processing so that salespeople could talk to databases such as Salesforce. During the first three months, the leadership was increasingly caught up in a mood of euphoria as they dreamed of all the money they were about to make. But then, suddenly, they decided that what we were building was too complicated. Panic swept over the company, and most of the work we'd done during those three months was thrown away. A new vision developed, a simplified product idea. This catalyzed another wave of euphoria, and then the cycle repeated.

In this particular case, the startup was led by salespeople who loved to do demonstrations for potential customers, but they never showed the customers the actual product we had. Instead, they showed an idealized vision of what the product might be in the future. On one hand, it was great that the leadership went out and talked to real customers. On the other hand, it was problematic that they never showed the real product. This actually exacerbated the euphoria-to-panic cycle, as customers would get very excited by our ideas — but then our estimates of when we'd be done building the prototype would get pushed out by six months and the leadership would sink into panic again.

My point is, if you feel fear about failing, that is completely natural. The way to avoid the aforementioned cycle is to talk to real customers. If you can find the humility to show people your unfinished, less-than-perfect work, their feedback can help you get out of your own head and focus on what's real.

There is no garden-variety company, so focus on your own unique needs

Dan Morena is co-founder and CTO of FundThatFlip. com, a very successful startup which finances speculative real-estate investments. The way he managed to keep costs down is a master class on the right way to make decisions at an early-stage startup.

In any design, the most daring decisions are often about where we say "no." And when it comes to FundThatFlip.com, Morena aggressively said "no" to many things that almost any other CTO would have said "yes" to.

Let's look at his most unusual decision. When they were just fledgling, Morena decided to host their online service with Heroku. By itself, that is not an unusual decision. Many startups begin with Heroku, because it's a cloud service which specializes in exactly that: making it easy to get started.

Here's the thing: Heroku is a bit inflexible. It also lacks many of the backup services and fail-over redundancies that are offered by more full-featured cloud services such as Amazon's AWS or Microsoft's Azure service. So a fairly common evolution for startups is that they commence with Heroku, and then if they are successful, they eventually move to a bigger cloud service.

But Morena refused to move. Seven years later, they are still on Heroku. Astonishingly, he currently spends less than $3,000 a month on cloud services, while his company handles over $100 million in loans. (By contrast, I've had clients spending over $400,000 a month on AWS.)

Dan Morena is a good friend of mine, so I've had the chance to talk to him about this unusual choice.

Me: Are you really sticking with Heroku?

Morena: For now. It keeps things simple. That means my team can focus on adding new features instead of focusing on supporting a bunch of complex configurations for different web servers.

Me: But don't you want to have a service that is reliable?

Morena: Heroku has been reasonably reliable. It gave us what we needed, especially in the early days. And if we keep our expectations limited, it still does what we need.

Me: You must have lost some business when it was down. I know it's had some occasional downtime. Aren't you losing business every minute your service is offline?

Morena: Well, not exactly. If someone has found a good real estate target for a flip, they've probably been doing research for months. If our service is offline for an hour, they will just come back later. No one is going to give up on a $2 million deal because they couldn't reach our service on the first try.

Me: Do you worry that some might think your attitude is unprofessional?

Morena: People have to understand the whole context. Especially in the early days, we didn't have much money, so I had to do what was simple and cheap. If I'd done what my peers considered "professional" then we would have burned through all of our money and shut down, so no one would have ever heard of us, and you and I wouldn't be having this conversation right now. We'd be just one of those startups that burned hot for a year or two and then disappeared.

Me: But you could have a much more reliable service if you had multiple, redundant systems that you'd be able to fall back to in an emergency.

Morena: Yes, but that would cost more. In many different ways. Heroku is simple, we never have to think about it, and that means that every time I hire a new software developer, that software developer can focus on building new features that our customers will love. That software developer does not have to waste time thinking about infrastructure and devops, so Heroku allows us to move fast, and to focus on giving customers what they want. Maybe, at some point in the future, we will move to AWS, but we need to think about it carefully. If we spend $1 million setting up some complex set of redundant services, what does that $1 million actually buy us? Does it buy us more sales? No, probably not. Seriously, what do we get in return for that $1 million? We get more reliability. Okay, great, so now what do we get in return for that reliability? Just more complexity for the tech team to manage, and therefore the need for a bigger staff, a staff that won't be building features for our customers.

Me: What if Heroku gets worse? I mean, hypothetically.

Morena: I have to base my decisions on what I actually know. If Heroku gets worse, then we'll move somewhere else, But I'm not building a hypothetical business; I'm building a real business. I can't make strategic decisions based on hypotheticals.

Me: You must realize that, given your scale, most CTOs

would consider it a matter of professional "best practice" to move to a full cloud service like AWS? The average company would have moved to AWS years ago.

Morena: They can do that at their company, but not at mine. Every company is different. There really isn't any "best practice" that works across all organizations indiscriminately. Some companies really do need redundant high availability, but our service does not. And every CTO needs to focus on what their company needs, not what the professional average is. There is no average, garden-variety company. Each company is unique.

Morena's focus on the real facts helps keep him grounded. Every decision goes back to what he knows about his customers. As a political matter, it probably helps that he is both a founder and the CTO, because if he was simply a hired-hand brought in to lead the tech team, he might feel more pressure to conform to generic, unspecific "best practice" professional standards. Investors might be more comfortable hearing, "We switched to AWS and that solved all of our problems," rather than, "We stuck with Heroku, come hell and high water." But Morena doesn't care. He knows what is working for his company, and that's all that matters to him. He is boldly anti-perfectionist: he knows he is losing some good qualities, such as reliability, for the sake of simplicity. He is daringly comfortable with what he gets in exchange for the sacrifice. He gets a beautiful simplicity, which allows his team to move fast, and, crucially, allowed his company to survive the early years, when they didn't have the money to build a complex system. FundThatFlip.com is doing well because of the surprising decisions he made.

But what does it look like when the top leadership doesn't have a grip on the real facts of the situation?

Realistic visions versus escapist daydreams

The eternal question, for entrepreneurs, is this: what notions do you have in your head that will lead to someone actually giving you money? If you are the creative type, you probably have some outlandish ideas that other people might find odd. But are those ideas a mere indulgence of your ego, or do they have business potential?

In his book, *The Lean Startup: How Today's Entrepreneurs Use Continuous Innovation to Create Radically Successful Businesses*, Eric Ries emphasizes the importance of the "minimal viable product," a product which only has enough features that you can then go and validate your hypothesis. Why waste money developing something no one wants?

Yet I've seen many entrepreneurs who get caught in endless development. Why? Often, it's because they are afraid of what potential customers might say to them. And why are they afraid? Let's look at a specific case.

When you are part of a brilliant team, can you be sure you were the reason for the team's success?

When I met him, Kennu was CEO at his second startup. His reputation was legendary. Unadulterated success followed him everywhere. He seemed to have the golden touch of Midas. He'd been part of the leadership team of an earlier startup that had done very well.

At one point we caught up with each other at Mistral, out in Princeton, New Jersey, near where he lived. He filled me in on some of the details about his life that I hadn't previously known. Apparently his success went far back. Even as a teenager he'd been a natural leader among his peers, admired and sought after. A leader of various organizations in college.

Now married, he spoke with some nostalgia of the ten years that he and his wife had enjoyed before their first child: two weeks in Japan, six months in Australia, a summer in Kenya, a month in Brazil, a year in Paris. She was working as a consultant, which gave her reasons to travel, while he was working on an Internet startup and could work from anywhere.

His current startup, which I'll call PrivacyBlockchain, was working on ways to use blockchain technology to help people manage their data privacy rights. In the same way we've become, over the last 60 years, a civilization that depends on people's credit scores, Kennu was dreaming of a happy future in which his startup would be just as indispensable, a crucial utility that all corporations and governments would need to consult to find out whether or not they were allowed to access someone's data.

Okay, I thought, very interesting, but where is the roll-out to the public? It's a good thesis for a product, but as Steve Blank said in his book *Four Steps to the Epiphany*, it is important to get a product into the hands of real users to find out if they actually find it useful. So where were the users?

I'd already met with his tech team multiple times. I was deeply concerned about what I saw going on — not because the technology was bad, but paradoxically, because it was too good. They'd built a fantastic technology a year ago, and then instead of showing it to potential customers, they just kept building. Why?

Early on they'd hired Robots & Pencils, one of the best software development agencies in New York City. After a few brainstorming sessions, a spec was drawn up, and work began. And they built. And they built. Everything about the product was excessively great. I realize that is a strange criticism to make, but the financial penalty of pursuing such excessive greatness was considerable. Kennu had raised $5 million for this startup and had spent more than $1 million on software development, all without showing the product to any potential customers. In what possible sense is that a "minimal viable product"?

I want to emphasize — the developers at Robots & Pencils are brilliant, and they built excellent software. Nothing that I write here is any way a criticism of their work. I only question the decision Kennu made to postpone the moment when the software was shown to potential customers.

"We need to be reliable," said Kennu. "What if *we* end up being the main way that people keep control of their medical data? What if we become the main enforcement mechanism for people's rights under HIPAA? People have to know they can depend on us."

Okay, that's a beautiful vision for the future. Maybe one day the whole country would depend on PrivacyBlockchain to help defend everyone's HIPAA rights. But is this the correct way for an entrepreneur to think? Maybe one day they will be worth billions of dollars. Maybe. For that matter, maybe one day the founders of PrivacyBlockchain will all be beautiful and loved and famous and own private islands in the Caribbean. I mean, if we're going to dream, then we might as well dream big, right?

But there is something dangerous about these kinds of dreams.

Over the previous year, Kennu had conversations with the lead engineer at Robots & Pencils. Here is an example of one of those conversations.

Kennu: This service needs to be highly reliable.

Lead engineer: Highly reliable? So, if the main service fails, we should have a redundant backup we can switch to?

Kennu: Yes, let's set up a redundant backup, in case of emergencies. Actually, let's set up two, in case a backup fails.

Lead engineer: You want two redundant backups? That seems excessive. We could write "relaunch the service" code that could get a new service up and running quickly, so you'd never have more than a minute or two of downtime.

Kennu: We cannot have two minutes of downtime, not ever, so let's have two redundant backup services running at all times. But yes, I like your idea, let's also write the "re-launch the service" code, so if both of our redundant back-up services fail, we can relaunch the service quickly.

Lead engineer: This is multiple layers of redundancy.

Kennu: Yes, good. We need this service to be reliable.

Lead engineer: I see. So we will want redundant databases as well?

Kennu: Yes.

Lead engineer: And redundant API gateways?

Kennu: I want everything to be redundant.

Lead engineer: Fortunately we are running on AWS, so it is easy to spin up a lot of redundant services.

Kennu: But what if AWS fails?

Lead engineer: That would be unusual.

Kennu: But it happens sometimes?

Lead engineer: Occasionally there is a problem in one re-gion, but we can follow a multi-region strategy. That way if a data center in one region has a problem, your service will automatically switch to a different region.

Kennu: But what if there are problems with multiple AWS regions simultaneously?

Lead engineer: That is very, very rare.

Kennu: But it could happen?

Lead engineer: Anything could happen.

Kennu: We need this service to be highly reliable. Can we also use other cloud services, like Microsoft's Azure service, and Google's cloud service?

Lead engineer: A multi-cloud strategy? Yes, we can do that. It's ambitious.

Kennu: But it can be done?

Lead engineer: Yes, we'd be happy to set that up for you. I've never done it before, so I'd be excited for the chance to try it.

Kennu: Great, let's do that! Anything to make the service reliable.

This is how more than $1 million got spent on what was more of a "maximal viable product" than a "minimal viable product." Outwardly, Kennu could claim that he simply had high standards and he was holding his product to the same standard as everything else in his life. Inwardly, what other than fear would cause someone to repeatedly delay showing the work to customers?

To be clear: when you have a big company, a stable product, and a stable revenue, then it is wise to invest money in redundant fail-overs to make sure the service is both reliable and secure. But doing this before you launch — when you have no idea if anyone is going to like your service — is the kind of perfectionism that should have your team asking, "Why are we doing this?"

A leader is made naked by their spending decisions

A leader is made naked by their budget. As President Biden has said, "Show me your budget, I'll show you your values." For a CEO, nothing speaks louder than how they spend their investor's money. Every dollar invested in a product, before the first dollar comes in from a customer, is a dollar that announces, "The CEO doesn't think this product is ready for customers yet." And your investors have the right to know why.

One problem with success at a young age is everyone then expects you to go on being successful. After all, a brilliant first act might have merely been luck, so people wonder, can you do it a second time? For someone like Kennu, the question lingered — had that first success been because of him? Or was it someone else on the leadership team who had produced that previous miracle? Maybe Kennu had no real talent, maybe he'd simply been in the right place at the right time? Some doubt haunted him.

Working as a consultant means that I am sometimes a kind of therapist. I've rarely seen a startup fatally sabotaged by a rational but incorrect assumption; typically a rational entrepreneur will simply pivot and go in a different direction, if their initial hypothesis is proven incorrect. What I've seen more commonly is startups sabotaged by something less explicit, something more difficult to put into words — inchoate fears and non-rational motivations. For this reason I wanted to get to know Kennu outside of the office.

It was a hot summer day when we met. We sat outside but in the shade. The food at Mistral, as always, was excellent. It was a chance for us to discuss things besides the business.

"I'm working on a novel," said Kennu, catching me a little off guard. "It's a science-fiction thriller."

"A novel?" I asked, surprised and curious. "What is it about?"

"A woman who signs away all of her rights, accidentally, one contract at a time, clicking 'Accept' on too many agreements without reading them."

"Interesting," I said. I, too, have written some fiction, so here was something we had in common. "How far have you gotten?"

"I'm done," he said. "I'm working with an editor to clean up the rough draft."

"Can I read it?" I asked.

"Sure, I'll send it to you."

Over the next weekend I read it over and drew up some detailed notes for him, commenting on every scene that I thought was good and every scene that needed improvement. I think he was surprised to get such thorough commentary; he seemed appreciative.

Like a lot of science fiction set in the near future, it started with an interesting premise. We all click "Accept" on various software agreements, and most of us click on these without actually reading the agreements. So, what if in the future it were possible to lose all of our rights by clicking "Accept" on too many of these agreements?

What I told him was that the first half of the novel was original and interesting, but the second half became too much of a standard action novel, with the main character trying to escape from an evil corporation and a bunch of guards shooting guns at her. My sense is that Kennu had an interesting premise for a story, but he didn't know how to end it.

Rather than focus on the details in the book, however, for our purposes it is more interesting to ask how a busy CEO found the time to write a novel. At the very moment that he should have been in the field talking to potential customers about his new service, he was sitting at home imagining an alternate reality.

Partly, I think he wanted people to know that he was creative. He wasn't just an average business guy who looked good in a suit. He had range. He wanted the world to see him as he saw himself. All of which is understandable. But branching out into new activities is typically what people do after they've sold a company, not while they're arduously trying to get a new company off the ground. Behind his dazzling smile there must have been a certain amount of personal burnout going on, a kind of emotional exhaustion that left him unwilling to focus on the next consecutive steps his startup needed.

The crucial question was whether he was aware of this himself. When I suggested that the novel must have taken up a lot of time he could have put into his startup, he simply deflected the point and said that he had time for everything. I found that response dishonest and worrisome. No one has time for everything, and he was smart enough to know that. Time is our scarcest resource; how we spend it says everything about what we are trying to achieve in life.

But here's another thing: great science-fiction can influence how we think about certain issues. Isaac Asimov wrote *I, Robot*, and it influences how we think about the machines we build – do they serve us or do we serve them? Ray Bradbury wrote *Fahrenheit 451*, and it influences how we think about censorship. Was Kennu writing his science-fiction story to influence how the public thinks about our loss of privacy? But wait, I thought Kennu's new service was going to solve that problem ...?

So this was the deepest conundrum: on some level, Kennu was having doubts about whether the blockchain could really solve all of the modern era's problems with loss of privacy. Every time he talked about the issue in any detail, he found himself thinking that Congress would have to change the laws to give citizens more rights to control their data. There was a limit on how much Kennu could do while the current laws were as slack as they were.

This is crucial to keep in mind: what he was facing is something that every entrepreneur faces. He'd started with a great idea, then he found out that his original idea wasn't going to work as well as he'd hoped. Yet there was still a lot he could do to help certain kinds of customers better manage their private data. I'm aware of at least six other startups that have made progress in this area over the last three years. Kennu would simply have to pivot towards a smaller demographic with particular concerns. Perhaps he could focus specifically on medical data, where the law is reasonably strict.

A CEO is buffeted by many forces. The investors are perhaps too loyal to the original vision, and you've already hired a team with specific skills to work on that idea, and that team is sometimes terrified of any shift in direction, as some of them perhaps don't have the skills to work on whatever the new idea might be. How should a CEO proceed? It's simple: by going out and talking to potential customers. They are the north star, the place to which the compass points, the only real source of truth to whom a CEO at an early stage startup should listen. Who is going to give you money in exchange for what product or service? Focusing on concrete details and specific questions is a great way to escape the vague fears in your head and get back to what's real.

Over the months, I got to know the whole staff. They were a smart crew, and they seemed to know the best bars in Manhattan. A whiskey sour has been my go-to drink for many years, and they made a good one at the bar at the NoMo SoHo hotel. That was where the head of marketing and the head of operations liked to meet. I have fond memories of chatting with them; they were both intelligent and funny. At the same time, I wondered if perhaps we were all having too much fun. While we had some great conversations, we were not making great progress on the business.

At one point, I left the NoMo at 11 PM and headed home. The head of marketing and the head of operations were still there. The next day we had a 9 AM meeting with Robots & Pencils, but both the head of marketing and the head of operations wrote to me around 8:45 AM to say they couldn't make it, one saying he was sick and the other claiming a family emergency. I cannot overstate how shocked I was. I like a good drink as much as anyone, but in my entire life I've never missed an early meeting because of something irresponsible I'd done the night before. These two were offering paper-thin excuses that I don't think anyone really believed. So I was left wondering: is this the level of professionalism on the team? Is this the level of discipline to be expected? Who hired these people? Would there be any consequences? In the end, the CEO must take responsibility for all of it.

Kennu is one of the most intelligent and creative people I've ever worked with, so I don't doubt he will eventually discover success for his startup. The path forward for Kennu might be difficult, but the basic steps are clear:

- Talk to potential customers. Find the humility to listen, even if they are critical of your original idea.
- Find a niche or specific demographic where your basic technology could be better applied.
- Warn your staff that it is forbidden to speculate about what customers might want. Actual conversations with high potential customers or actual customers are the only things that should matter.
- Fire any of the staff who are resistant to the new path, or whose skills are inappropriate for the new direction.
- Restrict spending. Only invest in the product when multiple customers have told you they need something specific. Do not waste any more money on speculative ideas.

Before any of that can happen, Kennu needs to get his head in the game. He cannot discipline his team if he himself is unfocused. Either he overcomes the burnout he is feeling, or he needs to resign his position.

Some of you might be wondering why I am telling such a

personal story. Isn't this a bit unusual for a business book? But my point here is that personal factors are also business factors. Indeed, when it comes to the early stages of a startup, personal factors dominate over all else. This is why I emphasize the psychological traits in the top leadership. I've known many entrepreneurs who obsess about the competition they might face in the marketplace, and yet the majority of all the startups that I have ever worked with have been undermined by the insecurities of the founders. I know for a fact that many of the people I once worked with could have become fantastically wealthy, but they got in the way of their own success. If we are going to have an honest conversation about the path to wealth, we need to talk about the emotional factors, the inner tensions, that sometimes sabotage otherwise great enterprises.

When entrepreneurs manage to stay focused on the needs of their customers amazing things can happen. Let's now look at an example of excellent customer focus.

Customer feedback isn't enough; there needs to be a structured way to prioritize that feedback

Lyndsey Allard and Kristen Giovanniello both had many years of experience researching customer responses. They knew that careful interviews with actual customers and potential customers can involve tedious ethnographic surveys, followed by more time combining those surveys into actionable data. Allard and Giovanniello knew the whole gamut of obstacles that tended to block the cycle of research and feedback, and they wondered, isn't there some way to automate some aspects of this work? This is how they first came up with the idea for their startup, PlaybookUX.com, which they started in 2018 and launched to the public in 2019.

Right from the start, they were able to find a market niche

and expand. Because they'd been doing this work for so long, they understood their ideal customer — someone similar to themselves, doing the work they had just spent most of ten years doing. Their marketing pitch was almost exactly what they themselves had wanted someone to offer them: "Watch participants provide verbal feedback while recording their screen. There's no limit to what you can test. Test anything, on any device. PlaybookUX allows you to validate your assumptions to make informed decisions. We'll point out key insights so you know what to add to your product roadmap."

Even that doesn't really explain all that they offer. For instance, they've found some excellent demographics to serve as their testers. One of their customers, a product manager, said with surprise, "Whoa, your testers actually write things! Like, they offer real feedback, they write full paragraphs. That's amazing. How did you find these people?" In previous years, many product managers, all over the world, have tried to use other services, such as Amazon's Mechanical Turk, to get feedback. They found the experience frustrating, at least in part due to the inconsistent and demotivated demographics who participate in those other services.

There is a cliché which says the intensity of a startup can put stress on the various friendships and relationships that exist among startup founders, but I find it more accurate to say that the stress of building a startup uncovers exactly how strong or weak a bond really is. Allard and Giovanniello had been dating since college, but if anything, building a business together brought them even closer together. In the summer of 2021 they got married.

When I asked Allard if the long hours of work ever left her feeling burned out, she said, "It helps that I'm doing this with Kristen. She is, obviously, my favorite person in the world. I'm not sure what this would be like without her."

Their startup was just beginning to get momentum when, in early 2020, the Covid-19 global pandemic briefly threatened to shut them down. Businesses of all types froze all purchase decisions for a few months. But then the world thawed, and it turned out the crisis was a gift for PlaybookUX. As businesses suddenly shifted most work out of the office, any software that could help with remote product development and customer testing became essential. For Allard and Giovanniello, the question became how to manage rapid growth.

Among the unusual decisions they made was an avoidance of investors. A different set of entrepreneurs might have taken their fast growth and used that to attract venture capitalist money, but for Allard and Giovanniello the most important thing was to maintain complete control over their own product.

"It's been interesting," said Giovanniello, "Some of our competitors who have taken VC money are not doing as well as we are doing."

"Because of the pressure to produce big profits quickly?" I asked.

"That could be it," said Giovanniello, "By contrast, we've taken our time with PlaybookUX. We wanted to get it right. And we wanted to expand on our own schedule. We don't want to be under pressure to expand artificially."

Without massive VC money to fall back on, they've had to be careful in their management of cash flow, and therefore they've had to be especially careful how they prioritized each new feature they added to their service.

"Two years ago we introduced a customer request log," said Allard. "Any time any customer makes any request, we log it. We made a conscious decision not to release that log to customers. I know a lot of companies do have a public facing log, where customers can go and upvote a feature request. Actually, not just a customer, anyone in the world can go and upvote some idea for a feature. But is that a good idea, to let anyone vote on a feature? If they are not a customer, if they are not spending money on the product, it's a little too easy for them to upvote a feature, even though that feature won't necessarily convert them into being an actual customer. So, this was a big decision for us — we decided we were not going to release our log to the public.

There were a few reasons why we did that. In terms of what our next step is going to be, or what our next feature will be, the decision to keep our log private makes our conversations easier. We can just focus on what actual paying customers have requested."

"You want to prioritize requests from real customers," I said, "not random requests from random people on the Internet."

"Exactly," said Allard.

"So, when you have all of these requests from real customers, how do you decide what to work on first?" I asked.

"We face the next question, which is how much time will a given feature take to implement?" said Allard. "Is it quick and easy? Is it high value? Or is it more like, hmm, this is something customers want, but it's going to take us a long time to build, so is it worth it? What is the impact, how much does it really help PlaybookUX to be able to say that we have this particular feature? Is this a 'nice to have' feature or a 'need to have' feature? This is a big part of how we make decisions."

"You must have a very long list of features that you'd like to build," I remarked.

"Yes, and we're self-funded," said Allard. "For a long time we prioritized customer value, that is, what they will see and pay for. For our first two years, every new feature was customer facing. If the customer wasn't going to see it, then we just skipped it. Everything else on the backend was manual. There were a lot of features that we could imagine that would make our life easier as entrepreneurs, as business owners, but we didn't build any of those features, because they were not customer facing. And I'm really glad that we did it that way, because once we finally started allowing ourselves to build some of the backend features, to help us automate some of our work, we realized, wow, if we had tried to automate things in the beginning, we would have made many wrong decisions. How we would have automated things is not how our customers would have wanted us to proceed. It's easy to start with some incorrect assumptions. For instance, thinking, 'Oh, people want this, or they don't want that,' — but we end up being wrong. So we waited, until we reached a scale where now we really need to automate. And now that we're finally automating some backend tasks, we can focus on fixing those things that are high risk."

"Can you give me an example?" I asked.

"As an example, what if someone asks for a receipt?" said Allard. "We use Stripe to handle money. I can go into our Stripe portal, but right next to the receipt button is the refund button. So that's high-risk. What if we refund money accidentally? That's embarrassing because then we have to re-charge them. And why am I doing this? Should we hire someone to send out receipts? No, we don't want to be training someone to do something that should, eventually, be in the customer-facing product. So, we decided, let's move that to the product, so the customer themselves can hit the receipt button. That is, we built a button that our customers can see, and they can click on that, and then in the background our code interacts with Stripe, and then our code renders a receipt for the customer. I was doing that manually, but we can move that from Stripe to our product and then let the customer fetch the receipt themselves. But did we understand the importance of this when we were starting? No."

She offered another example. "We allow customers to have a pre-paid balance. And then every time they run a study, we need to deduct some money from their balance. But, again, I was doing that manually, and there was room for mistakes. So what if I deduct the wrong amount? From our customer's point of view, any time we get the money wrong, that's a very bad customer experience. That might be unlikely and therefore low risk, but the impact is awful when it happens, so now we're putting in more controls around money."

I was again reminded that there is no "average" company; there are no generic "best practices" that work for every startup. Every company is unique and has unique needs.

"I notice that you're organically figuring this out, based on the unique circumstances of your company," I said. "I mean, you're a business-to-business startup, you only have a few hundred customers. So, you could handle receipts and refunds manually, for two years. If you were consumer facing, and if you had tens of thousands of customers, it never would have been possible for you to do any of these things manually. You would have needed to automate all of it before you first launched in 2019."

"Right," said Allard. "But we have certain strengths we can rely on. Within this industry, even for business-to-business — while we're an affordable solution, we're not a $5 solution. Most of our customers are paying us a few hundred dollars a month or more. So, that's enough that it pays for us to do some things manually, at least at first. Kristen and I are 'do it yourself first' people. Not with software development, of course, we don't have those skills — but for everything on the business side, we like to do it before we hire someone else to come in and do it. So we did everything for a while, before we started hiring people to do these jobs for us. It's useful to have done a job ourselves, because then it becomes easier for us to evaluate people when we hire for a given job. We know what's needed."

"But how do you decide to divide up the work?" I asked.

"Partly, that's been a process of figuring out what we are each best at," said Allard. "So, for instance, at first we tried to do all the work equally. But, take for instance, writing a blog post to announce a new feature that we just rolled out. Kristen is just better at that than I am. Writing a blog post is difficult for me. Kristen is more of a writer. So now she does that work. But meanwhile, for instance, I do more of the sales, the direct contact with customers, because that's easier for me."

Know your unique strengths: you are not running an average startup, you are running *your* startup

To summarize, here are some of the key habits that have allowed PlaybookUX to grow from strength to strength over the last three years:

- careful management of cash
- only log feature requests from actual customers
- a laser focus on those features that have the biggest impact for paying customers
- a nuanced system for weighting customer requests against the expense of implementing the requested feature
- doing most tasks themselves, before hiring people to do those tasks
- learning each other's strengths and weaknesses and then specializing their focus on the basis of their strengths

While there is no set of ideas that will work for every startup, every entrepreneur can still learn from the success of other entrepreneurs and borrow the ideas that seem most likely to help. What's important is to think creatively about how other people's good ideas can be adapted to one's own unique circumstances.

Beyond this specific list of specific habits that proved useful, there is a mindset that is deserving of imitation. Allard and Giovanniello don't waste much time dreaming about how great life will be once they are billionaires. They have a pragmatic mindset that keeps them focused on the present. And the present is where the success or failure of any startup will be determined.

In the 22 years I've been working with startups, I've rarely seen two entrepreneurs get as much right as Allard and Giovanniello. They've managed to grow and stay focused despite the extraordinary stress and isolation that was imposed on them by the arrival of a global pandemic. Their story is deserving of careful study, and my full interview with them is available online:

http://www.smashcompany.com/business/
interview-with-lindsey-allard-and-kristen-giovanniello

I believe their style of pragmatism can be learned by anyone who is serious about learning it. What is important is for entrepreneurs to have the humility to realize when they need to learn something. Indeed, the worst kinds of self-sabotage that I've seen in business have been from entrepreneurs who wanted to believe that they already knew all they needed to know.

The cosmic visions of a very boring man: humility versus delusions of grandeur

Why do so many startups flop? 90% of all such projects die. Even when based on brilliant ideas, the hard work and creativity of the team often comes to naught.

Emotions matter. We might hope that those in leadership positions possess strength and resilience, but vanity and fragile egos have sabotaged many of the businesses that I've worked with. Defeat is always a possibility, and not everyone finds healthy ways to deal with the stress.

In a large company, an eccentric individual does not do much damage. Even when such a person is in a leadership position, the company will have a bureaucracy that can ensure some stability. But when a company consists of only a few people, and one of them reacts neurotically to challenges, that company is doomed.

I'll relate one of my past experiences to illustrate this point. From 1999 to 2002, I created some software that could be used to create weblogs and other kinds of sites. Then in 2002 I teamed up with a man I'll call Timothy. We created a company together. He had inherited some money and seemed eager to invest in software like mine. Typepad.com, which offered something similar to what I'd built, had just raised $23 million in funding and was growing rapidly. Surely we could do the same?

Before I met him, Timothy had admired musicians and considered the music industry glamorous, so he built a sound studio, out in Nelson County, Virginia. The studio never made money. The bands that stopped by were broke. The few who came up with a hit song mostly signed with a major label which, typically, had its own recording studio. The most famous band that ever stopped by was Wilco, and I was pleased to meet them and listen to their recording session. But in order to get them to come out to the countryside and record at his studio, Timothy had offered to record them for free. He was hoping that he could then say, "We recorded Wilco," and it would help bring in other, paying bands. This never happened.

Working with him was difficult. We might go like maniacs on some project for four months, and when we were on the brink of unveiling it to the public, he would turn against it and insist we move on to some new project. The first time this happened he offered a reason that sounded plausible, suggesting there was too much competition in the space we'd targeted. But this pattern, where he walked away from a project right when we were ready to introduce it to the public, repeated itself a number of times. What led to this self-sabotage?

The Narcissist's Dilemma: every idea I have must be amazing, because I am amazing

Over the years, as I met Timothy's whole family, I got to see the sad dynamics that ate at him. He had a desperate need to impress his father. A modest business success would not be enough; in fact, it would leave him embarrassed. Only the creation of something as big as Google would satisfy. But to grow that big, we would first need to be small, and that was the step he had no patience for.

As the years went by, and he burned away all the money he'd inherited, the stress wrecked him. His self-image became increasingly grandiose. He told people that he was a visionary, someone who was able to tell what the future would look like. Late at night he would smoke marijuana and read articles on

Slashdot and TechCrunch and then put together an amalgam of words that seemed full of the bright hopes of humanity, which he offered up as our marketing: "The Universe is fundamentally electromagnetic yet non-sentient, and we are sentient but only partly electromagnetic; the Internet is the ultimate harnessing of sentience to the fundamental forces of the Universe. Therefore our software will put you, our customer, in the driver's seat of real-time conscious human evolution." Later, when he wrote up our business plan, he put these two sentences in the Executive Summary. I'm not joking.

He had no ability for internal dialogue. Only by talking to others could he hear his own thoughts. At our peak in 2007, we had eight people on our team. Sometimes I would look around the room, when he was talking at everyone, and I would think, "If you add up what we pay all these people, we are spending $300 an hour so that he can have an audience." When he felt fear about our chances of success, he would need to talk to everyone, and when he was euphoric about our chances of success, he would need to talk to everyone. Therapy would have been cheaper.

We had one modest success, in 2007. His girlfriend, a yoga instructor, suggested we build an online marketplace where yoga instructors could sell videos as well as offer health advice. This site was an immediate success. Within the first month it was profitable. We were written up in all of the major yoga magazines. It seemed obvious to me that we should use the same technology to build a series of similar sites. We could do a site devoted to cooking videos, another devoted to tennis, another devoted to golf. Indeed, just a few years later, the team behind Revolutiongolf.com did exactly what we could have done.

My business partner, however, was enraged by the success of the yoga site. He had burned through several million dollars chasing ideas that he felt were "visionary" and then his girlfriend came up with a simple idea that turned into our one true hit. To this day, it remains a popular yoga site. We could have built an empire around that site, but instead his girlfriend's success left him bitter.

Alfred Einhorn invented Novocain and then campaigned against its use by dentists

Perhaps I should have been prepared for Timothy's reaction. I'd read Peter Drucker. His book, *Innovation and Entrepreneurship*, is like a bible to me. And Drucker included a long chapter on the tendency of entrepreneurs to destroy the innovation they'd created.

Drucker relates the story of Alfred Einhorn, who invented Novocain, which became popular with dentists as a local anesthetic. Einhorn held a contempt for dentistry, since it represented such a small niche of medicine. He felt that Novocain should be used by surgeons for all forms of surgery, and so he waged a campaign against the use of Novocain by dentists. In the end, his innovation was successful despite him, rather than because of him. According to Drucker, this pattern, where a product or service is undercut by the entrepreneur who is trying to promote it, is extremely common.

By contrast, in 1961 Procter & Gamble introduced a new shampoo called Head & Shoulders. It helps reduce dandruff, thanks to the active ingredients of selenium disulfide and piroctone olamine. But 18 other shampoos were introduced around that time, and several of them also contained the same active ingredients. What made Head & Shoulders unique was its name and marketing, that is, its open embrace of the fact that it was for a particular niche demographic: people who had dandruff. The other shampoos, even the ones with selenium disulfide and piroctone olamine, were chasing after the broader market. From that era, the only shampoo that survives is Head & Shoulders. By focusing on a small niche, it was able to gain a foothold in a crowded market. Once it was established, it was able to branch out and offer other specialized shampoos, treating a variety of conditions, all offered by a brand that had become popular. It eventually became the leading shampoo in over 180 countries. It takes a certain discipline and humility to start with a small niche, yet that is often the path to big success.

Are you lucky or smart?

When I first read Drucker's book, I found it hard to believe that an entrepreneur would actively sabotage their own innovation. However, having now spent many years working with startups, I've seen that it is, indeed, a common pattern. Many entrepreneurs start companies at least in part because they consider themselves uniquely creative and insightful, and they want the whole world to see them as they see themselves. But reality may then prove them wrong. Perhaps their insights are proven false, perhaps what works in the end is something unexpected. For instance, in 1992, when Bo Peabody launched Tripod, he was thinking that the site would offer content aimed at college students. His idea failed. The company was saved because some of the software developers had started a side project that allowed anyone to create their own web pages. This then became the future of the company. In his book, *Lucky or Smart*, Peabody says it is important to be smart enough to know when you are getting lucky. And then, you have to be willing to accept that luck. What's needed in an entrepreneur is emotional resilience, the kind of strength that allows for openness to the unexpected.

Self-destructive entrepreneurs sabotage their own success when they feel it's the wrong kind of success

Three times now I've seen an entrepreneur sabotage their

own project because it became successful for what they felt were the wrong reasons. This emotional resistance to success is nearly always precipitated by one of two factors:

1. The success is with a small niche. The startup was supposed to grow till it was larger than Google, and success with a small niche is, therefore, extremely disappointing. The niche might be big enough to potentially generate several million in revenue, but it won't ever be enough to catch up with Google.

2. The success is of a conventional type and, therefore, the entrepreneur regards it as boring. Perhaps the site was supposed to pioneer an altogether new style of interaction among humans, and instead the part of the site that becomes popular is of an older kind — for instance, the blog on the site becomes highly successful. The entrepreneur is then disappointed, maybe even angry, to be the owner of a boring success.

Here then are some fatal traps to avoid. Without open-mindedness about the type of success you may encounter, your startup is doomed. And without humility about the limits of your knowledge, your startup is doomed.

When you are in the middle of the struggle, it is difficult to see that you are failing

Given that the problems with Timothy are so obvious, you might wonder why I worked with him for six years. There were three main reasons for this. I was having fun; I was learning a lot (probably faster than ever before or since); and we had several modest successes, so it was easy to believe we were on the verge of some much larger success. Indeed, it is the partial successes that make it difficult to see that your company is demonstrating dysfunctional behaviors which limit its long-term success.

It's all much easier to realize a few years later, when you see it in retrospect.

From a wealthy family that could trace its history in Virginia back to the 1600s, Timothy was born with multiple advantages. His father was famous for setting up a winery, and also for his establishment of a state park, created partly out of land that his father had donated. Timothy's younger brother went into the arts and worked at the Virginia Museum of Fine Arts in Richmond, and he was regarded as a genius for assembling large shows built around a daring thesis.

I am sympathetic to the pressure that Timothy faced. Great things were expected of him. When he was 25, his aunt died and left him a few million dollars. If you're running a 100-meter dash, but you're allowed to start 50 meters in, isn't victory automatic? How could he fail? Moreover, many of his college friends had gone on to become the CEOs at various big ventures. When was he going to be the CEO of something big?

Yet the fear of failure tore him apart. Before I'd met him, he'd spent $750,000 on his music studio, and after I met him, together we spent $150,000 building a social network that could compete with MySpace (because Facebook hadn't yet caught anyone's attention). Then we spent $190,000 on a site which allowed people to build their own websites (a bit like a minimal version of what SquareSpace, Wix, and Wordpress later offered). For just $50,000 we built Accumulist, which was a better version of Digg. Around that time Digg was at the peak of its popularity, though it was later surpassed by Reddit. And of course, my blog software was something we came back to on four different occasions during those six years. We must have spent more than $250,000 on it, and if we'd only been consistent in our efforts, we might have precluded the space eventually taken by Tumblr. Certainly, we'd started a few years before Tumblr and that should have given us the advantage.

Seeing him burn through much of his inheritance, Timothy's father became distraught and sought advisors who could steer his son right. This is how we ended up talking to Donovan in the summer of 2006.

Back in 1967, Michael Donovan had founded Donovan Data Systems:

Donovan Data Systems (DDS) is the advertising industry's leading systems and software provider. It offers an exceptional range of business solutions that bring operating efficiencies to clients working in advertising agencies. In the rapidly evolving world of media, DDS is working in collaboration with clients and partners to identify, analyze and standardize business processes, to ensure that its clients benefit from unmatched execution, efficiency and interoperability with all industry players.

https://www.crunchbase.com/organization/
donovan-data-systems

Donovan is a bit of a legend, one of the early success stories of the tech industry. An incredible innovator of the 1960s, he and his team had figured out how to build a great database before Edgar Codd or SQL or any of the modern technologies were available. And they had to make their systems work on very large computers that lacked the power you'd nowadays find in your average digital watch.

With his top advisor following along, Donovan stopped by one day and we had a long chat about our business model. With excellent instincts, he honed in quickly on our main problem, which was our lack of consistency. We'd made a little money with one website and a little money from another, but we had not stuck with anything long enough to enjoy some kind of substantial breakthrough.

Donovan asked why this was the case, but he got no answer. Timothy evaded the question and poured his energy into discussing his newest idea which, he assured everyone, was going to be a huge success, absolutely huge, just a massive, massive success!

No one believed him. There was some problem, but it wasn't clear what.

Still, Donovan liked us. Thereafter he let his 15 year-old daughter, Logan, come over to our offices to serve as a kind of intern, so we had her help most days that summer. A brilliant girl with many good ideas, we joked that she would make a better CEO than Timothy. Actually, there were some days I told that joke but I was not kidding. (Incidentally, she is now CEO of her own company.)

During the quiet days between Christmas and New Years, we were invited to dinner at the house Donovan kept near Wintergreen resort. We drove over together — Timothy, his girlfriend Ellen, and I. Around that house the security presence was heavy, with two guards that I could see and possibly more who were hidden. More guards were inside, or perhaps they were servants of some kind? I think they were guards, because they did nothing all night except stand discreetly in the corners of the room and watch us. There were two members of Congress who were visiting that night, and I wasn't clear if the security was for them or for Donovan. If you travel by helicopter, Wintergreen is only 30 minutes outside of Washington D.C., so it is a popular spot as a weekend getaway for Congresspeople.

Banal conversations are forgotten, but embarrassing moments are forever — and sadly, my most vivid memory of that night is of an awkward moment which came near the end. Donovan jokingly teased Timothy about enjoying the brainstorming process more than the "find customers" process, and Timothy responded by launching into a monologue about the transformative nature of the Web and how old business customs were going to die out and be replaced by pure creativity. Left unsaid, but heavily implied, was the suggestion that Donovan's ideas about building a business were obsolete — thanks to modern technology, a visionary such as Timothy could make a living by brainstorming ideas, which could be instantly actualized as a product thanks to the collective power of the Internet to alter our understanding of reality.

One of the Congressmen smiled and asked, "So you just brainstorm ideas, and then someone will give you money for said ideas?"

"Almost," said Timothy. "See, all truly novel thoughts must begin with new categories, which must begin with not just new ontologies, but whole new *paradigms* of ontologies, including evolutionary organic folksonomies, so we are surfacing a new kind of subterranean consciousness every time we further expand the total terra cognita of cyberspace, a process by which we allow the real-time realization of people's needs, which can then be actualized as products and services."

"Oh really?" said the smiling Congressman, who perhaps heard some echo of 60s futurism in Timothy's words — or perhaps he was simply smart enough to hear the desperation. When we spoke of our work, our styles were exactly opposite. Because I had confidence in our projects, I preferred to use plain language to make them accessible to the widest possible audience. Timothy, on the other hand, preferred to hide what we did behind a torrent of buzzwords.

The Congressman blinked. "How old are you?" he asked. He was not rude or patronizing; he had a kind, warm demeanor.

"I'm 32," said Timothy.

"What?" asked his girlfriend.

"I'm 32," repeated Timothy.

"You're 32?" asked his girlfriend in an exasperated tone of voice.

"Am I 31?" asked Timothy, with a furrowed brow, suddenly confused.

Everyone at the table laughed. I was embarrassed for him but also for myself. Since I'd come with Timothy and I was his business partner, I was guilty, by association, of this stupidity.

"You don't know how old you are?" asked the Congressman.

"I'm 32," insisted Timothy, now with some anger.

"You're not 32," insisted his girlfriend.

"Are you sure?" he asked.

"Are you serious?" she asked.

"I'm not 33, am I?" he asked.

"Of course, you're 33," insisted his girlfriend, with annoyance. "We just celebrated your birthday."

"Am I?" wondered Timothy. Everyone at the table laughed again and the mockery finally got through to Timothy, so he felt something like embarrassment — at least enough that he wasn't sure how to talk his way out of it, which was unusual since he had previously managed to talk his way out of many awkward moments. "Oh yes, that's right. I guess I am 33. I thought I was 32. Or maybe 31. But I'm 33. We recently celebrated my birthday, when I became 33, but I'd gotten mixed up and I thought maybe I was 32, or 31, because we recently celebrated and I forgot, but now I remember and I'm definitely 33."

If you've ever wondered how you can destroy your credibility quickly and completely, here is a master class for you.

For years afterwards, I would wonder about why he felt the need to lie about his age. My best guess is that he had a rigid idea about what success in his life looked like. A substantial portion of his identity was attached to the sobriquet "young visionary." And how young is that? Perhaps 27 or 28 or even 30? 31 was pushing it, 32 was almost middle-aged, 33 was far beyond the pale. Like many before him, he was failing to adjust his identity as he grew older.

Every time I tell this story, someone asks why the girlfriend needed to call Timothy out, in front of such august company. All I can say is, this is the way they were. They were constantly sniping at each other, even in the presence of others. You might think this presaged some deep fault in the relationship, but in fact, they are still together today, 15 years later.

You don't need 20 years of therapy to fight your demons

In this chapter I've told two success stories and two failure stories. FundThatFlip.com and PlaybookUX.com are doing amazingly well, because their founders manage to remain clear-eyed and pragmatic about what their startups need. But the startups overseen by Keenu and Timothy continue to struggle, year after year.

The problems here are entirely psychological. Keenu and Timothy were not blocked by outside competitors; they were sabotaged by themselves. They could still achieve enormous success, if only they could change their mindset.

Do they require years of therapy to figure out the deep roots of whatever their psychological issues might be? I'll offer a two-part answer. On the one hand, therapy can be useful for many people. No one should ever feel ashamed about seeking therapy, as it can help us see our own self-destructive patterns and overcome them. On the other hand, for many entrepreneurs there is a shorter path to success, which involves finding the humility to go out and talk to real customers, listening to what they say, and then acting upon that feedback. Don't dream about the distant future; think about today. Build your business one day at a time. Put one foot in front of the other. Every time you find yourself overwhelmed with fear or stress, try to ground yourself by going back to the feedback that you've gotten from actual customers or high-potential customers. You can make progress, right now, today, if only you can focus on right now, today.

Ultimately, you might become extremely wealthy and even famous. All of that really can happen. All of your dreams can come true. But paradoxically, you are more likely to get there if you don't focus on that distant future. Instead, focus on today.

Other Resources

You may want to get direct coaching to help you become a better leader. Or perhaps you'd like yourself and all of your startup co-founders to receive training, or you've hired managers and you'd like them to get training.

––––––––

There are thousands of leadership coaches out there, but their quality varies a good deal. One organization, where I know the quality of some of the people, is Eagle's Flight, which offers experiential learning, with enacted simulations to help you game play specific situations, the better to understand about how you should act:

https://www.eaglesflight.com/

Alain Hunkins worked at Eagle's Flight for many years and then launched his own service. He is a dynamic presenter and you will earn a lot from him. He also has a book: *Cracking the Leadership Code: Three Secrets to Building Strong Leaders*.

At various points over the years I've worked with two truly excellent CTOs, one of whom was Mark Herschberg. I asked him who he recommends for leadership training and he responded: "Leadership development is like software development. We all might all be developers but game developers are different from web developers who are different from medical device developers. There's different type of leadership." Herschberg also has a book, and the website for the book is full of great resources:

https://www.thecareertoolkitbook.com/

On the media page he links to a number of podcasts many of which are formally about leadership.

Keyiarra Wright is someone who I've worked with who is possessed of significant leadership skills. She has worked as a coach in the education sector. I asked her who she would recommend and she responded:

"The leadership program I participated in was Connecticut based and called the Leadership Development Roundtable."

https://fivefrogsct.org/opportunities/
leadership-development-roundtable

"There is another leadership program my colleagues have attended. It includes Connecticut and NYC women folks. The program is called Tide Risers."

https://www.wearetiderisers.com

She also recommended these three books:

Good to Great by Jim Collins

Thanks for the Feedback by Douglas Stone and Sheila Heen

Managing Up and Across by Harvard Business Review

Finally, entrepreneurs keep asking me, "How much can people work from home? Is it better to work in the office?" Please see what I wrote on my weblog here:

http://www.smashcompany.com/business/what-work-can-be-done-from-home-what-work-needs-to-be-done-at-an-office

Acknowledgements

Editing:

The author is grateful to Natalie Sidner, who did much of the editing on this book.

Also, Kathryn Bertoni and Misty Vredenberg offered valuable feedback.

Graphic Design:

Many thanks to Leah McCloskey, who designed the book and created the cover.

Made in the USA
Monee, IL
15 April 2023

31918243R10120